BEFORE
THE
THRONE
OF GOD

Light for Your Path

The Light for Your Path Series is for women who desire to know, love, and serve God better. Each book is designed to nurture new believers while challenging women who are ready for deeper study. Studies in the series examine *books* of the Bible, on the one hand (look for subtitles beginning with *Light from*), and important *topics* in Christian faith and life, on the other (look for subtitles beginning with *Focus on*). The series blends careful instruction with active reader participation in a variety of study exercises, always encouraging women to live in the light of biblical truth in practical ways.

Two foundational studies explain why and how to study the Bible as the one perfect light source for your Christian walk:

A Book Like No Other: What's So Special About the Bible
Turning On the Light: Discovering the Riches of God's Word

Also available:

The Light for Your Path Series Leader's Guide
God with Us: Light from the Gospels
His Witnesses to the World: Light from Acts
A Believer's Guide to Spiritual Fitness: Focus on His Strength

BEFORE THE THRONE OF GOD

Focus on Prayer

Carol J. Ruvolo

P U B L I S H I N G

P.O. BOX 817 • PHILLIPSBURG • NEW JERSEY 08865-0817

Unless otherwise indicated, Scripture quotations are from the New American Standard Bible. Copyright by the Lockman Foundation 1960, 1962, 1963, 1968, 1971, 1973, 1975, 1977. Italics indicate emphasis added.

Printed in the United States of America

Composition by Colophon Typesetting
Cover design by Now You See it!

Library of Congress Cataloging-in-Publication Data

Ruvolo, Carol J., 1946–
    Before the throne of God : focus on prayer / Carol J. Ruvolo.
        p.   cm. — (Light for your path)
    Includes bibliographical references (p.).
    ISBN 0-87552-630-6 (pbk.)
    1. Prayer—Christianity. I. Title. II. Series.
    BV210.2.R88   1999
    248.3'2—dc21   99-26104

To my mother, Betty Boling,
who never ceases to pray for me
because she knows how much I need it.

CONTENTS

PREFACE
Welcome to the Light for Your Path Series
ix

INTRODUCTION
The Neighbor
3

LESSON 1
Thinking Right Thoughts About God
9

LESSON 2
The Great Privilege of Family
17

LESSON 3
Energy for a Worthy Walk
27

LESSON 4
How to Pray with Success
37

LESSON 5
The Priority of Worship
49

LESSON 6
The Power of the Name
59

Contents

LESSON 7
The Role of the Spirit
67

LESSON 8
Prayer and Stiff Kids
77

LESSON 9
Making Our Requests Known to God
89

LESSON 10
The Umbrella of Gratitude
99

LESSON 11
Great Expectations
109

LESSON 12
A Divine Blueprint for Prayer
119

LESSON 13
The Pervasive Power of Prayer
129

APPENDIX A
What Must I Do to Be Saved?
139

APPENDIX B
What Is the Reformed Faith?
145

APPENDIX C
A Sampling of Paul's Prayers and Prayer Requests
151

RECOMMENDED READING
157

Welcome to the Light for Your Path Series

The Light for Your Path Series is designed to help women learn how to glorify and enjoy God by living out their transformation in Jesus Christ. Each book in the series reflects the author's commitment to the Bible as the infallible, inerrant, authoritative, and entirely sufficient Word of God, and her conviction that Reformed theology is the clearest and most accurate restatement of biblical truth.

The series begins with two foundational studies centering on the Bible itself. *A Book Like No Other: What's So Special About the Bible* presents (in six lessons) the unique character of God's revelation. *Turning On the Light: Discovering the Riches of God's Word* provides (in seven lessons) an effective approach to studying the Bible. Combining these two books in a thirteen-week course will prepare new and veteran students to gain the most from the Light for Your Path Series.

The remaining studies in the series fall into two categories. "Light" studies cover particular *books* of the Bible (or sections of books, or groups of books such as the Gospels). These studies guide you through portions of Scripture, enabling you to understand and apply the meaning of each passage. You will recognize them by their subtitles, beginning with the words *Light from.*

"Focus" studies spotlight important *topics* in the Christian faith and life, such as prayer, salvation, righteousness, and relationships, and seek to show what the whole Bible says about them. These studies also stress understanding and applying biblical truth in daily life. Their subtitles begin with the words *Focus on.* Studying a combination of biblical books and topics will shed much-needed scriptural light on your walk with God. Both types of Bible study should be included in a "balanced diet" for a growing Christian.

The *Leader's Guide* that accompanies this series contains a complete description of the purpose and format of these studies, along with helpful suggestions for leading women through them.

Bible study is a serious task that involves a significant investment of time and energy. Preparing yourself to study effectively will help you reap the greatest benefit from that investment. Study when you are well rested and alert. Try to find a time and place that is quiet, free of distractions, and conducive to concentration. Use a loose-leaf or spiral notebook to take notes on what you read and to do the exercises in this study. You may also want to develop a simple filing system so that you can refer to these notes in later studies.

Approach Bible study as you would any task that requires thought and effort to do well. Don't be surprised if it challenges you and stretches your thinking. Expect it to be difficult at times but extremely rewarding.

Always begin your study with prayer. Ask the Lord to reveal sin in your life that needs to be confessed and cleansed, to help you concentrate on His truths, and to illumine your mind with understanding of what He has written. End your study with a prayer for opportunities to apply what you have learned and wisdom to recognize those opportunities when they occur.

Each lesson in these studies is followed by three types of "Exercises": "Review," "Application," and "Digging Deeper." The *review* exercises will help you determine how well you understood the lesson material by giving you an opportunity to express the key points in your own words. The *application* exercises encourage you to put your understanding of the material to work in your daily life. And the *digging deeper* exercises challenge you to pursue further study in certain key areas.

You should be able to find the answers to the *review* questions in the lesson material itself, but please resist the temptation to copy words or phrases out of the lesson when you answer these questions. Work at putting these ideas into your own words. When you can do this, you know you have understood what you have read. It might help to ask yourself, "How would I explain this idea to someone else if I didn't have the book with me?"

If you don't have time to do all of the *application* exercises, pray over them and ask the Lord to show you which one(s) *He* wants you to work on. Because you will be applying the lessons to your daily life, these applications should take some time and thought. Answering one of them well will benefit you more than answering all of them superficially.

Answers to the application exercises should be very specific. Work at avoiding vague generalities. It might help to keep in mind that a specific application will answer the questions Who? What? When? Where? and How? A vague generality will not. You can make applications in the areas of your thinking, your attitudes, and your behavior. (See lesson 6 of *Turning On the Light* for more about application.)

Digging deeper exercises usually require a significant amount of time and effort to complete. They were designed to provide a challenge for mature Christians who are eager for more advanced study. However, new Christians should not automatically pass them by. The Holy Spirit may choose to use one of them to help you grow. Remember that *all Christians* grow by stretching beyond where they are right now. So if one or two of these exercises intrigue you, spend some time working on them. And do not hesitate to ask for help from your pastor, elders, or mature Christian friends.

As you work through this study, resist the temptation to compare yourself with other Christians in your group. The purpose of this study is to help you grow in your faith by learning and applying God's truth in your daily life—not to fill up a study book with brilliantly worded answers. If you learn and apply *one element* of God's truth in each lesson, you are consistently moving beyond where you were when you began.

Always remember that effective Bible study equips you *to glorify God and enjoy Him forever.* You glorify God when you live in such a way that those around you can look at you and see an accurate reflection of God's character and nature. You enjoy God when you are fully satisfied in His providential ordering of the circumstances in your life. When your life glorifies God and your joy is rooted in His providence, your impact on our fallen world will be tremendous.

Behold the Throne of grace!
The promise calls me near:
There Jesus shows a smiling face,
And waits to answer prayer.
—John Newton

The Neighbor

*G*eri *picked up a stack of freshly laundered towels and turned toward the hall linen closet when she heard someone tapping on her front window. A quick glance revealed the face of her neighbor, Janet, smiling at her through the glass. Shifting the towels to one arm, Geri smiled in return and waved her friend in.*

"Is this a bad time?" Janet asked, eyeing the towels and the open laundry room door.

"Are you kidding? I was looking for an excuse not to do any more laundry." Geri chuckled and extended her free arm to give Janet a hug.

"Oh, look out!" Janet cried as the leaning tower of towels suddenly buckled and fell to the floor.

"Well, well," Geri winked at her friend as they both set to work retrieving and refolding. "Now I have two excuses to quit doing laundry!"

Ten minutes later the women were seated in Geri's cheerful blue-and-white kitchen, sipping hot tea, and easily chatting. During the first quiet moment, Janet cleared her throat and put her cup down.

"Could I talk to you about something?" she asked hesitantly and immediately looked down at the table.

"Sure." Geri put her own cup down and looked straight at her neighbor.

"It's a little embarrassing, but I need your help."

"Take your time." Geri leaned in toward Janet and spoke to her gently. "You know I'll help if I can."

Janet took a deep breath and looked up at Geri. "Do you remember about a month ago when Cathy asked me to pray at Bible study, and I said I wasn't feeling very well, so would she please ask someone else?"

Geri nodded. "That was the first time she asked you to pray, wasn't it? . . . Oh, Janet, I'm sure Cathy would understand. A lot of people don't like to pray out loud in groups."

Janet shook her head and looked down again. "That's not it, Geri. I'm not shy, and I don't suffer from stage fright." She raised her head and swallowed hard. "I went home that day realizing that I don't know how to pray out loud. In fact, I wasn't sure if I knew how to pray at all. So I decided it was high time that I learned. I went to the bookstore and bought about a dozen books on prayer. And I read every one of them."

"No wonder I haven't seen much of you during the last month!" Geri smiled and leaned back in her chair. "Did it help—all that reading?"

"Not really. Now I'm so confused that every time I try to pray, I freeze up completely." Janet looked a bit sheepish but more relaxed. "There were so many different ways to pray in those books. I must have written down five or six different formulas—and of course, each one was guaranteed to work. A few authors said that prayer was just talking to God and didn't need any structure at all. One man said if I didn't have enough faith, I'd never get what I wanted—but if I did have the faith, I could claim anything from God and He would be obligated to give it to me. Another man said that I shouldn't ask God for things. He said that God does what He pleases and all prayer does is help me submit." Janet paused and looked at Geri. "Do you see why I'm confused?"

"Yes, I do."

"I had a feeling you would. That's why I came to see you this morning. You see, I've heard you pray—and I know you're good at it. So I thought you could tell me which of those books are right. Which ones should I keep, and which ones should I toss?"

"Janet, I don't know which of those books you should keep. But I do know of another good Book on prayer. In fact, it's the only Book that I trust completely. Would you be willing to go through the Bible with me and see what our Father God says about prayer?"

If you are like me, you identify with Janet. You have been through times in your Christian life when prayer seemed like a mystery you couldn't unravel. Perhaps you are going through one of those times at this very moment. But even if you are one of those stalwart prayer warriors like Geri who seem to have the mystery of prayer solved, when you are alone before God, you too long to know more about this blessed privilege.

God wants us to pray because we are His children. He established this glorious means of two-way conversation to strengthen the family bonds that tie us to Him and to each other. Prayer opens our eyes to God's glory, our hearts to His will, and our needs to His perfect provision. It reveals, solidifies, and confirms the unity of the Spirit that we share with other Christians. And it keeps us alert to the wiles of the Enemy. Prayer is essential to a walk worthy of our high calling in Christ.

So why do so many of us find it so difficult? Why are we embarrassed to pray aloud in a group? Why do we hesitate to pray in public? Why are we simply too busy to make it to prayer meeting? Why do we wonder if we are "doing it right"? Well, perhaps we are sinning. Or, perhaps we are simply unlearned or untrained. Or, perhaps, like our friend Janet, we are confused.

Fortunately, the solutions to every one of those problems are easy to find. God has told us in His Word *all* that we need to know about prayer and our practice of it. He has even provided clear-cut examples for us to follow. The Bible is our perfect guidebook to the great blessing of prayer.

In the thirteen lessons that follow, we will open that guidebook together and ask God's Spirit to teach us to pray. We will seek His encouragement, direction, and wisdom, and then we'll practice His truth until it is engrained in our natures. By the time we are finished, we should have not only a better understanding of prayer but a better prayer life as well, one that is

> filled with the knowledge of His will in all spiritual
> wisdom and understanding, so that [we] may walk
> in a manner worthy of the Lord, to please Him in
> all respects, bearing fruit in every good work and
> increasing in the knowledge of God; strengthened
> with all power, according to His glorious might, for
> the attaining of all steadfastness and patience; joy-
> ously giving thanks to the Father, who has qualified
> us to share in the inheritance of the saints in light.
> (Colossians 1:9–12)

I am deeply grateful to the following saints of God who have contributed greatly to my understanding of and de-votion to prayer: my mother, Betty Boling, and her friends at New Covenant Presbyterian Church (Anderson, S.C.), whose effective, fervent prayers on my behalf have ac-complished so much; my pastor, Randy Steele, who has worked hard at teaching his flock how to pray directly from Scripture; the devoted prayer warriors in my Wednes-day night fellowship group who committed themselves to practice what Randy was teaching us; my dear friends Blair, Elaine, Patti, Mike, Randy, Rick, Lisa, Deanna, Mark, John, Marlene, Barbara, Thom, and Karen, whose much-coveted prayers encourage me more than I'm sure any of them realize; and the great God and Father of our Lord Jesus Christ who hears and answers all the prayers of His children.

1

Thinking Right
Thoughts About God

We are to pray with an awful apprehension of the majesty of God. —Westminster Larger Catechism, Q/A 185

How good a theologian must you be to pray good prayers? The answer, which may surprise you, is that you must be quite a good one.

"Now wait just a minute," I can hear you say. "I know some *children* who pray excellent prayers!"

So do I. And I would submit that those children are very good theologians. You see, being a good theologian doesn't require advanced degrees. It doesn't require reading thick books or understanding big words. It simply requires thinking right thoughts about God. And *that* is essential to praying good prayers.

Good Prayer Needs an Anchor

Some time ago my pastor explained to our Wednesday night fellowship group why he thought we needed to practice praying directly from Scripture. He told us that we are most likely to slip into poor theology in *prayer* because we are used to praying "unanchored"—that is, with God's Word out of sight and (worse) out of mind.

Perhaps you grew up (as I did) with the idea that good prayer is essentially spontaneous, informal, and "free" from constraints. If so, may I challenge you (as my pastor did me) to reconsider. What I learned from nine months of praying directly from Scripture was that, whereas good prayers may well be spontaneous and informal, they are never really "free from constraint." Good prayers grow out of thinking right thoughts about God. And thinking right thoughts about God demands that we *anchor* our minds in the bedrock of Scripture.

When we cut our prayers loose from the secure moorings of Scripture, we increase the risk of their becoming vain, self-centered, and earthbound. Praying with God's revealed truth out of sight and out of mind usually produces requests that reflect *our will,* not His. Ironically, such prayers are never truly free. True freedom comes when we present ourselves to our Father as His "slaves for obedience" (Romans 6:16), not when we seek His power to fulfill *our* wishes.

True freedom in prayer is enhanced as we *practice* praying directly from Scripture with the Holy Spirit's assistance. The Spirit works through His Word to help us praise God, confess sin, and make our needs known *with eternal priorities in mind.* Prayers that are anchored in eternal truth free our souls from the tyranny of vain, temporal, and selfish concerns.

One thing I have learned from my enjoyment of traveling cross-country by rail is that trains move most freely when they are constrained by the tracks. They aren't nearly so free when derailed and bouncing across the prairie! In order to get anywhere, a train must operate within the confines of its design. And prayer is no different. Since God designed prayer as a blessed means of communion between Himself and His children, it works best when confined to the revealed truth of Scripture.

"Open-Book Prayer"

When I was in school, I always did much better on "open-book" tests than on tests that required me to rely solely on memory. Perhaps that's why I began referring to our Wednesday night gatherings as times of "open-Book prayer." I found I was praying much better with the Bible open before me than I did when relying on my poor, fallible memory. Praying directly from Scripture kept me from thinking wrong thoughts about God and helped me pray with more confidence.

Good prayer is essential to a walk that is worthy of our high calling in Christ. It encourages us to strive earnestly to fulfill the ultimate purpose for which we were saved (Philippians 3:12). It focuses our attention on God's revealed will as we "press on toward the goal for the prize of the upward call of God in Christ Jesus" (v. 14). Prayer also delights us, consoles us, calms us, and thrills us by helping us set our minds "on the things above," not on the things of earth (Colossians 3:2).

John Blanchard reminds us that good prayer "substitutes man's weakness with God's strength, man's ignorance with God's wisdom, man's emptiness with God's fullness, man's poverty with God's wealth, man's impotence with God's omnipotence."[1] What great motivation to pray with right thoughts about God!

Saul, What Were You Thinking?

The flip side, of course, is that thinking *wrong* thoughts about God is harmful to prayer. King Saul learned that lesson firsthand when his wrong thoughts about God interfered with his prayers and cost him his kingdom.

God had instructed the king to "strike" and "utterly destroy" the Amalekites (1 Samuel 15:3). But Saul thought that God would be happy with partial obedience. He struck the Amalekites, as God had told him, but failed to follow through with their utter destruction. Instead, for what he *thought* was a very good reason, Saul spared Agag, the Amalekite king, and "the best of the sheep, the oxen, the fatlings, the lambs, and all that was good" (v. 9).

Saul explained his thinking to God's prophet Samuel: "The people took some of the spoil, sheep and oxen, the choicest of the things devoted to destruction, to sacrifice to the LORD your God at Gilgal" (v. 21). But Saul's wrong thinking nullified both his worship and his service as king. Samuel answered pointedly,

> Has the LORD as much delight in burnt offerings
> and sacrifices
> As in obeying the voice of the LORD?
> Behold, to obey is better than sacrifice,
> And to heed than the fat of rams.
> For rebellion is as the sin of divination,
> And insubordination is as iniquity and idolatry.
> Because you have rejected the word of the LORD,
> He has also rejected you from being king."
> (vv. 22–23)

In response, Saul continued down the road of wrong thoughts by neglecting prayer altogether. Note that he asked forgiveness and pardon from *Samuel* instead of from God (vv. 24–25) and was sternly rebuked by the prophet: "I will not return with you; for you have rejected the word of the LORD, and the LORD has rejected you from being king over Israel" (v. 26).

Wrong thoughts about God not only do damage to prayer; they also produce unhappy circumstances.

Wrong Thoughts About God Amount to Idolatry

We can see from King Saul's example that God does not condone wrong thinking about Him. That's because wrong thoughts about God amount to idolatry. They substitute a "god" we have fabricated (with our minds instead of our hands) for the God of Scripture and transfer the reverence that we owe Him to a pretender.

The first four of the Ten Commandments prohibit the making of idols and require that we worship God alone. God also affirmed through the prophet Isaiah His exclusive right to our single-minded devotion: "I am the LORD, that is My name; I will not give My glory to another, nor My praise to graven images" (42:8). And He used the mouth of another prophet, Habakkuk, to declare the utter futility of idolatry:

> What profit is the idol when its maker has
> carved it,
> Or an image, a teacher of falsehood?
> For its maker trusts in his own handiwork
> When he fashions speechless idols.
> Woe to him who says to a piece of wood,
> "Awake!"
> To a dumb stone, "Arise!"
> And that is your teacher?
> Behold it is overlaid with gold and silver,
> And there is no breath at all inside it.
> But the LORD is in His holy temple.
> Let all the earth be silent before Him. (2:18–20)

Mental idolatry is just as offensive to God as is bowing down to a piece of carved wood. Therefore, we should strive to be good theologians in prayer by making sure our thoughts about God are anchored in Scripture.

Notes

1. John Blanchard, *Truth for Life: A Devotional Commentary on the Epistle of James* (Durham, England: Evangelical Press, 1986), 32.

Exercises

Review

1. How good a theologian must you be to pray a good prayer? Explain.

2. Explain why good prayer is never free of constraints. Then explain why prayer that is free of constraints can never truly be free.

3. Do you think that praying directly from Scripture necessarily eliminates spontaneity in prayer? Explain.

4. Define the phrase "open-Book prayer." How might it help you think right thoughts about God?

5. List several motivating reasons to pray with right thoughts about God.

6. Read 1 Samuel 15 and describe how Saul's wrong thoughts about God affected his prayers. What were the consequences of Saul's poor theology?

7. Explain why God takes wrong thoughts about Him so seriously. Can you think of other areas of life besides prayer that are affected by thinking wrong thoughts about God? Describe these affects.

Application

1. *Open-Book Prayer:* Every day this week during your prayer time, base your praise and worship of God on Psalm 145 and Isaiah 40:9–31.

2. Consult several reference books about prayer, including the relevant sections of a few theology books, and record as many different definitions of prayer as you find in them. Then locate (using a concordance if necessary) and read six to ten actual prayers recorded in the Old and New Testaments of the Bible. Which of the definitions you recorded best describe these biblical prayers? Explain why they do. Select the definition you think best describes the prayers you read (or write your own definition) and commit it to memory. Then answer the following questions:

   How do your prayers compare with the ones you read and with your selected definition? Cite specific examples of how they are both similar and different.

   What changes should you make in order to bring your prayers more in line with Scripture? List these changes.

   Make a detailed plan to implement these changes and ask a friend or a relative to hold you accountable to your plan.

Digging Deeper

1. Study the events recorded in Genesis 4:1–16, Leviticus 10:1–20, Deuteronomy 12:1–32, 1 Samuel 15:1–31, Jeremiah 10:1–25, and Acts 8:4–24. Use these events to describe how a person might intend to worship the true God, but in fact be engaging in idolatrous worship. According to these passages, how does God react to such behavior? How does your study of these passages shape your attitude toward worship? Do you see any parallels between these passages and current trends in worship? If so, explain.

2

The Great Privilege of Family

Live as a child of God; then you will be able to pray as a child and as a child you will most assuredly be heard.
—Andrew Murray

Imagine the following scenario: Your oldest daughter and you have diligently depleted the family fortune at the local shopping mall and are rewarding yourselves with a treat at your favorite ice cream parlor. The task of selecting one (or maybe two) flavors from the tantalizing array of multi-colored, multi-textured, and multi-caloried frozen delights almost overwhelms you. But, as bold Women of the New Millennium, you step forward to name your respective poisons: Triple Nut Fudge Delight for you and Cherry Berry Bonanza for her.

The clerk skillfully tops two sugar cones with two generous scoops each and hands them to you. You, in turn, hand them to your daughter to hold while you pay. Your daughter runs her tongue around the luscious pink mound of her Cherry Berry Bonanza and rolls her eyes in ecstasy.

Then, with a sly glance in your direction, she samples your cone as well. "Oh, that's good," she exclaims. "You wanna trade?"

Now imagine a different scenario: The clerk skillfully tops two sugar cones with two generous scoops each. But before handing them to you, *he* tastes each one and says with a sigh, "Two of my favorite flavors!"

Most of us would not be alarmed at the first scenario. But the second is different. If you're like most people, *your daughter* helping herself to your ice cream cone is no problem. She's family. She has privileges other people don't have. But when a stranger assumes privileges of family, he acts presumptuously. And that's a problem.

The same principle applies in the family of God. His children have been given the family privilege of prayer. Those outside the family don't share in that privilege. When they do pray, they presume a right they don't have, whether out of brashness or ignorance of whose family they're in.

Who Is Your Father?

In the eighth chapter of John, Jesus laid to rest the popular fallacy of the universal fatherhood of God and brotherhood of man. He was speaking to Jews who, although they had believed the truth of His teaching, had not believed *on Him* for salvation. Jesus angered them by declaring that their flawed belief excluded them from the family of God. "True disciples," He explained in verse 31, do much more than believe—they "abide."

The incensed Jews hotly reminded Him of their physical lineage in Abraham. But Jesus tersely informed them that they were in fact slaves of sin who had never gained freedom by faith in God's Son. Their desire to kill Him testified that His abiding Word was not in them and revealed that they were spiritual descendants of Satan, not of God's servant Abraham. "If God were your Father," Jesus forthrightly explained, "you would love Me. . . . Why do you not understand what I am saying? It is because you cannot hear My word. You are of your father the devil, and you want to do the desires of your father. . . . He who is of God hears the words of God; for this reason you do not hear them, because you are not of God" (vv. 42–47).

Jesus' words made it clear that not everyone can claim God as Father, nor all of humanity as brothers and sisters. There are two distinct families: one that we are all born into "naturally" and one into which we must be adopted.

Adopted by Covenant

Those who have been adopted enjoy the privileges of family not because they were born to them but because they were chosen. God has only one "naturally born" child in His family, the man Jesus Christ. All the rest of His children He has graciously chosen to be joint-heirs with this Son.

Although human adoption is often motivated by a perceived worth *in the child,* our adoption by God was much different. A. W. Pink explains that "the supreme end which God had in view was His own glory, the subordinate end the recovery of His lapsed and ruined people."[1] God secured us a place in His family entirely out of His holy desire to display His marvelous love, mercy, grace, and justice. And what a display our salvation is! "God demonstrates His own love toward us, in that while we were yet sinners, Christ died for us" (Romans 5:8).

For no greater reason than His own glory, God chose to reconcile to Himself a number of His enemies, thereby transforming them into His children. Those children love Him because He loved them first. He did all this at the cost of His only "naturally-born" Son (Romans 5:10). Jesus died in our place to satisfy God's wrath against our sin. He also lived a perfectly righteous life, which God credits to us. Because of these two acts of Christ, we are as precious in God's sight as His beloved only Son.[2]

Even more amazingly, our adoption was no mere afterthought of the Fall. It was planned and sealed in eternity past, when the Father, Son, and Holy Spirit covenanted together to bring it about. The *Son* became "incarnate," taking on human nature, so that He could live as a man in perfect obedience to God's law and bear the penalty of that law in behalf of sinners. In so doing He would offer to God an atoning sacrifice that would satisfy His justice, magnify His holiness, and win for His chosen children all the blessings of heaven.

The *Father* guaranteed His acceptance of the Son's work by raising Him from the dead and exalting Him to His own right hand. There He would rule over the world and intercede as Divine Advocate for His adopted joint-heirs. God justifies sinners and conforms them to Christ's image so that they can share eternity with Him. He does this by bringing about the divine exchange Paul describes in 2 Corinthians 5:21: "He made Him who knew no sin to be sin on our behalf, that we might become the righteousness of God in Him."

The *Spirit* witnessed and recorded the covenant and then assumed His role of applying it to each one whom He saves. He works in the depraved hearts of elect unbelievers to make them aware of their sin, willing to repent, and able to respond to God's grace with life-giving faith.[3]

The salvation brought about by this Trinitarian covenant did more than place us in a new family. It also changed our hostile hearts into hearts that love and respect our Father. As His children we naturally long to know Him more deeply. And one of the ways we can do that is by taking advantage of the family privilege of prayer.

God's Purpose for Prayer

In his book *Approaching God,* Steve Brown describes prayer as a "family kind of thing."[4] He says that God designed prayer primarily as a means of spending time with His children. Prayer is, therefore, not so much a means to some other end as a delightful and practical end in itself.[5] The prophet Isaiah expresses God's desire to commune with His people when he says,

> Therefore the LORD longs to be gracious to you,
> And therefore He waits on high to have
> compassion on you.
> For the LORD is a God of justice;
> How blessed are all those who long for Him.
> (30:18)

And David captures the heart of all who long for Him:

> One thing I have asked from the LORD, that I
> shall seek:
> That I may dwell in the house of the LORD all the
> days of my life,
> To behold the beauty of the LORD,
> And to meditate in His temple. (Psalm 27:4)

Prayer is a celebration of our family relationship with God. It allows us to respond to the miracle of our adoption in four glorious ways: (1) by expressing our gratitude for His graciousness, (2) by offering our praise of His majesty, (3) by confessing and seeking His cleansing of sin, and (4) by making our requests known to Him. As we acknowledge in prayer our childlike dependence upon God and learn to rely on His promise to supply all our needs according to His riches in glory, our relationship with Him grows deeper and stronger.

Growth in that relationship bears inevitable fruit. As we become increasingly oriented toward the goals of our spiritual family, we become ever more useful to the Father in accomplishing His purposes. And as we enjoy the privilege of being useful to God, we come to appreciate more fully the place of prayer in God's plan.

Prayer is indeed a "family kind of thing." God uniquely designed it to foster intimacy with His children and to accomplish His divine will. As such, it is a privilege reserved for believers, not some kind of "right" due to humanity in general.

Unbelieving Prayer Is Presumption

Scripture emphasizes the exclusive nature of prayer. John 15:7 declares, "If *you* abide in Me, and My words abide in you, ask whatever you wish, and it shall be done for you." John 9:31 adds forthrightly, "We know that God does not hear sinners; but if anyone is God-fearing, and does His will, He hears him." And the book of Proverbs says,

> The sacrifice of the wicked is an abomination to
>   the LORD,
> But the prayer of the upright is His delight. (15:8)

And,

> He who turns away his ear from listening to the
>   law,
> Even his prayer is an abomination. (28:9)

The Bible's declaration that God "hears" prayer refers to much more than His physical awareness of the words spoken. Because God is omniscient, He is aware of all words and all thoughts of all people at all times. But when God "hears" a prayer, He recognizes the voice of a child seeking the Father. Such prayers are consistent with His divine purpose for prayer, and God always responds to them in ways that fulfill His perfect plans for that child.

B. B. Warfield explains that the true prayers of God's children presuppose His existence, personality, accessibility, and continued activity in the world. He also says that all prayer that God *hears* comes to Him in faith through Christ Jesus.[6] The writer of Hebrews says, "He who comes to God must believe that He is, and that He is a rewarder of those who seek Him" (11:6). And the Lord promised His children through the prophet Jeremiah: "You will call upon Me and come and pray to Me, and I will listen to you. And you will seek Me and find Me, when you search for Me with all your heart" (29:12–13).

When reading these verses, remember that "seeking God" is quite different from "seeking from God" what you want. The first comes to God *on His terms* for His purposes, while the second arrives with a personal agenda. The first seeks God's face, not merely a handout. When unbelievers—who don't acknowledge His right to rule over them—"seek God in prayer," they approach Him as a source but not as a Sovereign, as a force but not as their Father. They reduce prayer to presumption.

Remember that God ordained prayer as a means of spending time with His children. He is not at all bothered when we take full advantage of our family privileges. But He is greatly displeased when those outside His family presume "rights" they don't have.

Notes

1. A. W. Pink, *Gleanings from Paul: The Prayers of the Apostle* (Chicago: Moody Press, 1967), 56.

2. Christ's satisfaction of God's righteous wrath against sinners is called "propitiation." Theologians use the word "imputes" to express God's act of crediting or ascribing Christ's perfect righteousness to us.

3. For a detailed discussion of this covenant of redemption, see O. Palmer Robertson, *The Christ of the Covenants* (Phillipsburg, N.J.: Presbyterian and Reformed, 1980).

4. Steve Brown, *Approaching God: How to Pray* (Nashville: Moorings, 1996), 146.

5. Ibid., 116.

6. B. B. Warfield, "Prayer as a Practice," in *Faith and Life* (Carlisle, Penn.: Banner of Truth, reprint 1990), 433–35.

Exercises

Review

1. Read John 8:31–47 in conjunction with 15:1–11 and explain the difference between the short-fall belief Jesus condemned in the Jews and the abiding belief He speaks of to His disciples. What do these passages tell you about the family privileges of believers?

2. Describe the responsibilities assumed by each member of the Trinity in the covenant of redemption that secured our adoption into the family of God.

3. According to A. W. Pink, what were God's two "ends" or purposes for salvation? How are these two purposes related?

4. Describe the "divine exchange" that occurs in salvation.

5. Explain why prayer is a "family kind of thing." As such, how does prayer strengthen the family of God and equip us for service?

6. Explain why unbelieving prayer is presumptuous. Support your answer with Scripture.

Application

1. *Open-Book Prayer:* In your prayer time this week, use Psalm 139, John 10:1–30, and Romans 8:28–39 to help you express your gratitude to God for adopting you into His family.

2. List some of the many privileges that are yours as a member of God's family, along with scriptural references to support them. Now list the responsibilities that go along with those privileges. Take these privileges and responsibilities to God in prayer, thanking Him for the privileges and seeking His wisdom and strength to exercise the responsibilities wisely.

3. Did you "pray" before you were a Christian? If so, describe how your prayers changed after you were saved. Give examples if possible. If you did not pray before you were saved, explain how your new activity of prayer reflected the change that has taken place in your life.

Digging Deeper

1. Andrew Murray has said, "Live as a child of God; then you will be able to pray as a child and as a child you will

most assuredly be heard." Using what you learned in this lesson as a basis for further research, explain the connection Murray is making between prayer and your *life* as a child of God.

2. Should an unbeliever's prayer of confession in seeking salvation be considered presumptuous? Explain your answer including scriptural support. How does this kind of prayer differ from "unbelieving prayer"?

LESSON 3

Energy for a Worthy Walk

Prayer was never designed to be a substitute for dili-
gence in keeping God's precepts, but is a means whereby
we obtain grace for obedient conduct. —A. W. Pink

Have you ever read through the book of Acts in one sit-
ting? If you haven't, try it sometime. When you do, imagine yourself trying to keep up with Paul on one of his mis-
sionary journeys. If your imagination is good, you'll soon
be exhausted. You may even find yourself wondering what
brand of vitamins fueled this nonstop apostle.

Paul was undeniably energetic. He never seemed to
grow weary in doing good (Galatians 6:9) or to flag in his
efforts to "press on toward the goal for the prize of the upward call of God in Christ Jesus" (Philippians 3:14). He trav-
eled extensively, preached extemporaneously, and wrote
prolifically—without the benefit of frequent flyer miles,
portable sound systems, word processing software, or
audio-visual equipment.

How did he do it? What was his secret? We can find out

by listening in on his prayers. You'll find most of them recorded in appendix C at the back of this book. Before going on with this lesson, turn there and read them carefully to see if you can detect the source of his energy.

Paul, the Apostle of Energy

Do you see how Paul got his unquenchable energy? Would you agree with me that it came from his consummate focus on the glory of God? Paul's prayers were uttered in the language of praise. They were punctuated with thanksgiving and formatted for service. They came from the heart of a man truly transformed by "the working of the strength of [God's] might which He brought about in Christ" (Ephesians 1:19–20). And they were addressed in humble confidence to "Him who is able to do exceeding abundantly beyond all that we ask or think, according to the power that works within us" (Ephesians 3:20).

Paul's prayers concern "the things above, not . . . the things that are on earth" because when he died to self, his life became "hidden with Christ in God" (Colossians 3:2–3). In response, God infused his ministry with everything that he needed for every good work (2 Corinthians 9:8; Colossians 1:29).

The energy that fueled Paul's worthy walk flowed from the depths of a soul intent on knowing and serving Jesus Christ. Paul expressed it this way to the Philippian church:

> For to me, to live is Christ, and to die is gain. . . . I have suffered the loss of all things, and count them but rubbish in order that I may gain Christ . . . that I may know Him, and the power of His resurrection and the fellowship of His sufferings, being conformed to His death; in order that I may attain to the resurrection from the dead. (Philippians 1:21; 3:8–11)

Paul's life was neither easy nor comfortable. He spent most of his time on the road or in prison, where he was "beaten times without number." He routinely faced dangers from rivers, oceans, cities, and the wilderness, as well as from robbers, his own countrymen, Gentiles, and false brethren. He labored in hardship, through sleepless nights, in cold and exposure, in hunger and thirst—all while also burdened for the welfare of the churches (2 Corinthians 11:23–28).

He was besieged by a cruel "thorn in the flesh," which God saw fit *not* to remove despite Paul's heartfelt entreaties. "My grace is sufficient for you," God told His servant. "For power is perfected in weakness" (12:9). Paul's response to God's hard-to-hear words uncovers the heart of his unflagging zeal: "Most gladly, therefore, I will rather boast about my weaknesses, that the power of Christ may dwell in me. Therefore I am well content with weaknesses, with insults, with distresses, with persecutions, with difficulties, for Christ's sake; for when I am weak, then I am strong" (vv. 9–10).

In other words, Paul was energized by his worship of God. What kept him going in good times and bad was, ironically, not his strength but his weakness. When he was weak, his thoughts and prayers were lifted up to the Almighty One, who answered by giving him sufficient strength in His Spirit to serve Him effectively. The power of prayer is affirmed in Paul's amazing endurance amid fierce opposition.

Paul, a Worthy Example

Paul wasn't shy about urging his readers to imitate his example (1 Corinthians 11:1; Philippians 3:17)—not because he thought more highly of himself than he should have, but because he himself followed the example of Christ. Paul prayed for the strength he needed for ministry because that's what his Lord did (Matthew 14:23; 26:36–46; Mark 6:46; Luke 5:16; 6:12; 9:28; 22:41–46; John 11:41–44). The apostle could not have found a better example. And neither can we.

God has called us to live in righteous contrast to the depraved world around us (Matthew 5:16; Ephesians 2:10; Titus 2:11–14). Such a life is undeniably stressful and requires a great deal of stamina. But since God is most glorified when we *enjoy* our life in Christ, He provides abundant energy for us through the gracious blessing of prayer (Hebrews 4:16).

Prayer has often been compared to the physical act of breathing. Both actions are prompted by the same type of distress. Just as the physical atmosphere around us puts pressure on our lungs and stimulates them to breathe, the spiritual atmosphere of our lives puts pressure on our souls and stimulates them to pray. The more effectively we breathe, the more we enjoy our physical existence. And the more effectively we pray, the more we enjoy our relationship with the Father.

Andrew Murray has said that effectual prayer is generated by complete consecration to the fulfillment of our calling and that the more effectual our prayers, the more we are blessed by them.[1] He adds that we enjoy a taste of heaven on earth when we surrender ourselves completely to God's perfect will for our lives. Such a life of service and obedience is the beauty and charm of heaven.[2] Paul's zest for life in "any and every circumstance" (Philippians 4:12) lends Spirit-inspired validity to Murray's comments.

Paul was in prison when he wrote his "epistle of joy" to the Philippian church. And since first-century prisons make those of today seem like country clubs, we know his physical circumstances must have been miserable. But Paul expresses contentment (v. 11) and even elation that his "circumstances [had] turned out for the greater progress of the gospel" (1:12). Such attitudes characterize one who habitually prays that "love may abound still more and more in real knowledge and all discernment, so that you may approve the things that are excellent, in order to be sincere and blameless until the day of Christ" (1:9–10).

Paul had learned by the Spirit to look at his life through the grid of God's eternal purpose and gracious provision. He knew that his God was righteous, holy, and good, and that he could trust Him to perfectly order all his circumstances.

How much more effectively would we fulfill God's purpose for saving us if we devoted ourselves to praying with Paul's godward attitude?

Prayer for a Worthy Walk

Why did the Holy Spirit inspire Paul to include so many of his prayers in his letters? Romans 15:4 gives us a clue: "Whatever was written in earlier times was written for our instruction, that through perseverance and the encouragement of the Scriptures we might have hope." Second Timothy 3:16–17 adds even more light: "All Scripture is inspired by God and profitable for teaching, for reproof, for correction, for training in righteousness; that the man of God may be adequate, equipped for every good work."

The Holy Spirit gave us a sampling of Paul's prayers to teach us and equip us for every good work. Both the teaching of the Bible and prayer itself are "means of grace."[3] God uses them graciously to produce spiritual growth in us, making us more like Christ.

Our Father knows that His children learn best when they have good examples to follow. Paul's prayers, as well as the other prayers recorded in Scripture, serve as excellent models for ours. As we follow these examples, we'll find ourselves praying—and walking—in a manner more "worthy" of our high calling in Christ.

Biblically grounded prayers help us walk in truth (3 John 3–4). They equip us to "walk by faith, not by sight" (2 Corinthians 5:7) as "children of light" (Ephesians 5:8–9) in whatever circumstances God has placed us (1 Corinthians 7:17–24). When we join with other Christians in patterning our prayers after biblical models, we become unified in our faith, "standing firm in one spirit, with one mind striving together for the faith of the gospel" (Philippians 1:27). Biblical prayers deepen our knowledge of God and His will (Colossians 1:10), and instill the wisdom we need to "[make] the most of [our] time because the days are evil" (Ephesians 5:16–17).

Confessing our sin and receiving God's promised forgiveness (1 John 1:9) help us to develop qualities of purity (Romans 13:13–14), humility (Romans 12:3), gentleness, patience, and love (Ephesians 4:1–3) that shine through our good works to the glory of God (Matthew 5:16; Ephesians 2:10). Our daily lives become increasingly characterized by a supernatural joy (Philippians 4:4–5) rooted in deep thankfulness for God's goodness (Colossians 1:11–12). His grace stimulates us to bear the fruit for which we were chosen (John 15:16).

When God gave us the priceless privilege of prayer, He opened an inexhaustible energy resource for ministry. But availing ourselves of its benefits requires serious effort on our part. We must study the instructions He has left us in Scripture and practice praying like those whose examples He has provided.

A. W. Pink expressed it well when he said,

> God has provided grace answerable to our every need, yet it flows through the *means* He has appointed. God will "perfect: stablish, strengthen, set-

tle" us in response to fervent prayer by the instrumentality of His Word, by His blessing to us the various ministries of His servants, and by sanctifying to us the disciplines of His providences. He who has given His people a sure hope will also give everything necessary for the realization of the thing hoped for (II Peter 1:3); but it is uniquely our part to seek the desired and necessary blessing by prayer (Ezek. 36:37).[4]

Notes

1. Andrew Murray, *With Christ in the School of Prayer* (Old Tappan, N.J.: Revell, 1953), 128.

2. Ibid., 129.

3. The "means of grace" are the media God has chosen to use in conjunction with the sovereign working of His Holy Spirit to enable His elect to receive the grace necessary for salvation and sanctification. The grace needed for salvation is received through Scripture, preaching, personal witness, and evangelism, whereas the grace required for sanctification is received through the exposition of Scripture, prayer, communion, and fellowship with other believers.

4. A. W. Pink, *A Guide to Fervent Prayer* (Grand Rapids: Baker, 1981), 146.

Exercises

Review

1. Describe the importance of energy in all areas of life.

2. Explain, in your own words, how Paul's all-consuming focus on the glory of God energized him for ministry. Cite specific examples from Paul's life as illustrations.

3. List several things we can learn from Paul's example about the purpose and practice of prayer.

4. How might prayer be compared to breathing?

5. Read through the short book of Philippians and describe how this "epistle of joy" supports Andrew Murray's assertions about prayer on page 30.

6. Explain how effectively using prayer as a means of grace helps Christians walk worthy of their high calling in Christ.

Application

1. *Open-Book Prayer:* In your prayer time this week, use Ephesians 3:14–19 or Colossians 1:9–12 to help you pray for your brothers and sisters in Christ; and use Ephesians 6:19–20, Colossians 4:2–4, and/or 2 Thessalonians 3:1–2 to help you pray specifically for your pastor and church leaders.

2. Read once more through the prayers and prayer requests of Paul recorded in appendix C. Highlight in your book, or record on a separate sheet of paper, recurring words and phrases in these prayers. What do these recurring words and phrases reveal about the *focus* of Paul's prayers? About his *overall attitude* toward and in prayer?

   Read through these prayers and prayer requests again before answering the following questions:

For whom did Paul pray?

What did he ask God to grant them?

For what was Paul thankful?

For what specific things did Paul request prayer for himself?

How do your prayers compare with Paul's? (Give specific examples of similarities and differences between your prayers and Paul's.)

Try praying more like Paul every day for two weeks and see if you detect an increase in your energy level for ministry.

Digging Deeper

1. Study the following biblical prayers (and any others you would like to include) along with the prayers of Paul found in appendix C: David's prayer described in 2 Samuel 12:15–23; Hezekiah's prayer in 2 Kings 19:14–19 (If you are not familiar with the situation that prompted this prayer, read all of 2 Kings 19.); David's prayer in 1 Chronicles 29:10–19; Daniel's prayer in Daniel 9:3–19; Jesus' prayer in John 17; the believers' prayer in Acts 4:24–30 (If you are not familiar with the situation that prompted this prayer, read all of Acts 4.). Describe the common focus and themes found in all these prayers, and explain what this exercise has taught you about God's primary purpose for prayer.

LESSON 4

How to Pray
with Success

*Prayer is beyond any question the highest activity of the
human soul. Man is at his greatest and highest when
upon his knees he comes face to face with God.*
                                        —D. Martyn Lloyd-Jones

From 1987 to 1993 I was privileged to minister with the
Biblical Counseling Foundation, a group committed to
helping fellow Christians live as "overcomers" by applying
God's Word to difficult circumstances of life. My primary
task was teaching a course called "Self-Confrontation."
The class covered basic principles of living and was required of all aspiring biblical counselors, as well as many
who came seeking counseling.

The twenty-two lessons in the Self-Confrontation man-
ual seemed, at first glance, to range randomly over a wide
variety of topics. They included evangelism techniques,
the sufficiency of Scripture, approaches to problem solving,
developing and maintaining good family relationships,
controlling anger, and overcoming "life-dominating" sins.

However, two underlying principles tied the whole class together: (1) Learning to live as an overcomer requires looking at our circumstances *from God's perspective* rather than our own. (2) Applying biblical truth in our lives involves *making specific step-by-step plans.*

As I taught Self-Confrontation several times over, those two principles embedded themselves firmly enough in my mind to support every step of my walk with the Lord. They have structured and strengthened my prayers, and have assured their success.

Praying with God's Perspective

Some of you may have "red-flagged" the last word in the previous paragraph. And if you did, I want you to know that I'm impressed. Your desire to have me define what I mean by "success" tells me that you *think* as you read—and that's impressive.

Steve Brown also thinks as he reads—and as he writes. And I have found no better definition of "success" in our prayers than his description of it as walking close to God and growing in holiness.[1] That definition harmonizes well with what we have already learned about prayer as a means of sanctifying grace. If we desire success in that sense (and we should!), we must come apart from the world and look at our circumstances from our Father's perspective. That humbling process underscores our complete dependence upon God while it mortifies our sin, thus drawing us closer to Him and developing holiness in us.

But how do we do that? A good way to begin is by asking ourselves some questions based on what God has told us in Scripture. For example, God has told us that we were created for His glory and to enjoy Him forever (Isaiah 43:7, 21; 1 Corinthians 10:31; Psalm 73:25–26). *What do we need to fulfill our created purpose?* He's told us we were predestined to become conformed to the image of Christ (Romans 8:29). *Do we play a part in that process, and if so, what kinds of things should we be doing?* God has told us that He has redeemed us from every lawless deed to purify us as a people for His own possession, zealous for good works (Titus 2:14). *What behaviors, attitudes, or things in our lives hinder us from becoming such people?*

God instructs us to deny ungodliness and worldly desires and to lead sensible, righteous lives in this present age (Titus 2:12). *How do we live like that in our fallen world?* He tells us to be careful how we walk, not as unwise men, but as wise, making the most of our time because the days are evil (Ephesians 5:15–16). *What habits of life would we be wise to change?*

God warns us not to think more highly of ourselves than we ought to think (Romans 12:3), but to put the interests of others ahead of our own (Philippians 2:3–4). *Have we allowed our self-absorbed culture to distort our thinking in this area?* And, He reminds us that since we have been raised up with Christ, we are to set our minds on things above, not on the things that are on earth (Colossians 3:1–2). *How can we keep a heavenly focus when we must make a living, fix lunches, wipe drippy noses, and scrub dirty bathrooms?*

These kinds of questions will help us unearth what we really need for a closer, more holy walk with God. As we seek God's perspective, we'll find ourselves praying with greater success.

What Do We Really Need?

When I was studying accounting at the University of New Mexico, I learned that wise business executives concentrate on long-term rather than short-term profitability. That's because the fundamental "need" of any successful business is maintaining its ability to operate into the future. All the other needs of the business are subordinate to that one. When business decisions become short-sighted, long-term profitability suffers and the future of the business is jeopardized.

This very same principle applies to a successful walk with the Lord. Jesus made it clear in one encounter with Mary and Martha that every Christian's most basic need is *knowing Him* (Luke 10:38–42). Since "in Him all the fulness of Deity dwells in bodily form, and in Him you have been made complete, and He is the head over all rule and authority" (Colossians 2:9–10), all of our other needs are subordinate to knowing Him.

Getting to know Jesus is the way we get to know God. Getting to know Jesus is the way we get to know we've been saved from His wrath against sin. And getting to know Jesus is the way we get to know the debt of love we owe our Father.

Thus, our "real needs" concern our relationship with God through His Son, Jesus Christ. Those needs are revealed to us in the pages of Scripture. And so, "successful" prayer depends upon understanding God's Word. Surely God's encouraging words to Joshua apply as well to our prayers as they did to the conquest of Canaan: "This book of the law shall not depart from your mouth, but you shall meditate on it day and night, so that you may be careful to do according to all that is written it; for then you will make your way prosperous, and then you will have success" (Joshua 1:8).

Since, as Isaiah 46:10 tells us, God will accomplish *all of His purposes,* assurance of success in any spiritual endeavor results from knowing that our efforts coincide with His ultimate purposes. One of those purposes is perfecting the good work He began in us through Jesus Christ (Philippians 1:6). God, in His wisdom, accomplishes that particular purpose by requiring us to "work out [our] salvation," while He effectively works in us "both to will and to work for His good pleasure" (Philippians 2:12–13).

Part of working out our salvation is identifying our real needs through a careful study of Scripture and then asking our Father to do His work of meeting them. Such prayers can be offered with confidence because Scripture also reveals that He will cause His grace to abound to us so that "always having all sufficiency in everything, [we] may have an abundance for every good deed" (2 Corinthians 9:8).

The New Testament writers encourage us to pray with such confidence. After exhorting us to "keep living by that same standard to which we have attained" (Philippians 3:16), Paul instructs us to "be anxious for nothing, but in everything by prayer and supplication with thanksgiving, let [our] requests be made known to God" (4:6). If we do that, he says, "the peace of God, which surpasses all comprehension, shall guard [our] hearts and minds in Christ Jesus" (v. 7).

The writer of Hebrews urges us to "hold fast our confession . . . [and] draw near *with confidence* to the throne of grace, that we may receive mercy and find grace to help in time of need" (Hebrews 4:14, 16). John adds, "And this is *the confidence which we have before Him,* that, if we ask anything according to His will, He hears us. And if we know that He hears us in whatever we ask, we know that we have the requests which we have asked from Him" (1 John 5:14–15).

In the book of Acts, Luke gives us an example of one such confident, biblically based prayer. Peter and John have just been released from prison after a dramatic confrontation with several Jewish officials. The two apostles have hurried home to tell their Christian friends what happened. The group turns the whole situation over to God—by presenting to Him their *real needs* defined in terms of His revealed truth:

> O Lord, it is Thou who didst make the heaven and the earth and the sea, and all that is in them, who by the Holy Spirit, through the mouth of our father David Thy servant, didst say,
>
> > "Why did the Gentiles rage,
> > And the peoples devise futile things?
> > The kings of the earth took their stand,
> > And the rulers were gathered together
> > Against the Lord, and against His Christ."
>
> For truly in this city there were gathered together against Thy holy servant Jesus, whom Thou didst anoint, both Herod and Pontius Pilate, along with the Gentiles and the peoples of Israel, to do whatever Thy hand and Thy purpose predestined to occur. And now, Lord, take note of their threats, and grant that Thy bond-servants may speak Thy word with all confidence, while Thou dost extend Thy hand to heal, and signs and wonders take place through the name of Thy holy servant Jesus. (Acts 4:24–30)

Was their prayer successful? Luke seems to think so:

> And when they had prayed, the place where they had gathered together was shaken, and they were all filled with the Holy Spirit, and began to speak the word of God with boldness. . . . And with great power the apostles were giving witness to the resurrection of the Lord Jesus, and abundant grace was upon them all. (vv. 31, 33)

Successful Prayer Needs Some Planning

Just as successful prayer depends upon our seeing circumstances from the perspective of God's purposes, it also depends on careful step-by-step planning. Few of us would question that any successful endeavor requires plenty of planning. Sturdy buildings must be erected from skillfully drawn blueprints. Functional and flattering clothing is made with the help of a pattern. Tasty, nourishing meals are created by carefully following recipes. And the salvation of God's elect is accomplished according to His plan of redemption. Why, then, would we doubt that effective prayer must be planned?

The basic purpose for planning (if I may mix a few metaphors) is to get all your ducks in a row so that all your bases are covered and nothing falls through the cracks. And one very good method of planning is to ask all-encompassing questions that demand specific responses. The best "matched set" of questions of which I am aware is the one used by journalists to get all the key facts of a story: Who? What? When? Where? Why? and How? Let's use them to see if we can develop a good plan for our prayers.

For whom should we pray?[2] Scripture is clear that we should pray for ourselves (Philippians 4:6; James 1:5–8), our families (Genesis 25:21; Numbers 12:13; Matthew 19:13–14), our political leaders (Ezra 6:10; 1 Timothy 2:1), our spiritual leaders (Ephesians 6:19–20; 2 Thessalonians 3:1–2), other Christians (1 Samuel 12:19, 23; James 5:16), the sick (James 5:15), the afflicted (Psalm 72:12–15), the lost (Romans 10:1), and those who persecute and mistreat us (Matthew 5:44; Luke 6:28).

For what should we pray? The well-known acrostic ACTS helps us identify the proper subjects of prayer. The letters in the acrostic, which stand for Adoration, Confession, Thanksgiving, and Supplication, remind us that successful prayer is much more than a recitation of needs. The exemplary prayers of the Bible focus intensely on praise (1 Chronicles 29:10–19; Psalm 19) and repentance (Daniel 9:3–19; Psalm 51) and are shot through with thanksgiving (Psalm 107; Romans 6:17–18; 1 Corinthians 1:4–9; 2 Corinthians 9:15; Ephesians 1:15–19; Philippians 1:3–5; Colossians 1:3–6; 1 Thessalonians 1:2–4; 2 Thessalonians 1:3; 1 Timothy 1:12–14; Philemon 4–6). Supplication (requests), the essential element of prayer on which most of us major, usually follows (and is therefore defined by) adoration, confession, and thanksgiving.

The emphases I have detected in the prayers of the Bible have led me to redesign the ACTS acrostic a bit. I have kept the same letters but rearranged them to spell TACS, written like this:

This new acrostic highlights the overarching, umbrella-like *attitude* of thanksgiving (Colossians 4:2) that permeates all prayer. And the respective sizes of the letters A, C, and S emphasize the priority of praise and repentance, which help us develop a godly perspective of needs.[3]

When and where should we pray? The Bible instructs us to pray in the morning (Psalm 5:3), at night (Psalm 119:148), three times a day (Daniel 6:10), and without ceasing (1 Thessalonians 5:17). It also teaches us to pray in private (Matthew 6:6) and in public (John 11:41–42), alone (Nehemiah 1:4–11) and in groups (Daniel 2:17–23). Obviously

God gives us much leeway regarding when and where we should pray—which makes planning to pray absolutely essential. A casual approach such as "I'll pray whenever I get around to it" rarely generates much prayer! Successful prayer requires designating specific places and times at which we'll meet God.

Select a time to pray when you are alert and well rested. And choose a place to pray where you will not be interrupted or distracted. Establish a prayer time long enough to keep you from rushing, but not so long as to tempt you with boredom or sleepiness.

Why should we pray? The most concise answer is that God has ordained prayer as an essential means of sanctifying His children in His gracious presence. The scope of this answer has been and will continue to be expanded throughout this book.

How should we pray? John MacArthur in his book *Alone with God* describes nine "biblical" postures of prayer and concludes that there is, therefore, no *one* right physical position.[4] However, Scripture does set some parameters regarding right *attitudes* in prayer.

Prayer should be God-centered (Matthew 6:9–13), reverent (Psalm 119:9–10), and confident (Hebrews 4:16; 1 John 5:14–15). It should be regarded as a serious task to be undertaken with intense persistence (as opposed to a demanding insistence) (Luke 11:5–8; 18:1–8) and a great deal of humility (Luke 18:10–14). Prayer should sometimes be accompanied by fasting (Matthew 17:21) and may at times require us to seek assistance from other Christians (James 5:16).

So how do we pray with success? The answer is simple but never easy to implement: Seek God's perspective on every aspect of life, and don't fail to plan.

Notes

1. Steve Brown, *Approaching God: How to Pray* (Nashville: Moorings, 1996), 81.

2. The question "Who should pray?" was answered in lesson 2; and the question "To whom should we pray?" could be correctly answered either with "Any and all members of the Godhead" or "God the Father, in the name of Jesus Christ, through the power of the Holy Spirit." These two answers will be explored more thoroughly in lessons 5–7.

3. The function of thanksgiving (or gratitude) in prayer will be discussed in more depth in lesson 10.

4. John MacArthur, Jr., *Alone with God: The Power and Passion of Prayer* (Wheaton, Ill.: Victor, 1995), 1.

Exercises

Review

1. Describe Steve Brown's measure of successful prayer. Can you think of a better way to measure success in prayer? If so, describe it.

2. How does looking at our circumstances from God's perspective rather than our own promote success in our prayers? What are some practical ways you can do this?

3. What is every Christian's most fundamental need? Explain why this is true. How is meeting this need dependent upon understanding God's truth in Scripture?

4. Identify the elements of the Acts 4 prayer that make it a good example of defining our needs in accordance with God's perspective of our circumstances. What did these believers identify as their real need in this situation? How do we know their prayer was "successful"?

5. Explain why successful prayer must be planned.

6. List and explain the major considerations involved in planning your prayers.

Application

1. *Open-Book Prayer:* This week in your prayer time, use one or more of Psalms 147–150 to help you praise God, Psalm 32 to help you confess your sin, and Matthew 6:9–12 to help you present your needs to Him. Meditate on Colossians 4:2 and Philippians 4:6 to help you maintain an attitude of thankfulness throughout all of your prayer times.

2. Spend some time identifying your own needs by meditating on the following Scripture passages and answering the questions associated with them as *specifically* as possible:

Psalm 73:25–28; Isaiah 43:7, 10–13, 21; Habakkuk 3:16–19; 1 Corinthians 10:31: What do you need in order to glorify God and enjoy Him in your *current* circumstances?

Romans 8:28–30; Philippians 2:1–16; 2 Timothy 3:1–16: Do you play a part in God's purpose of conforming you to the image of Christ? And if so, what do you need to play that part well?

Romans 12:1–21; Ephesians 4:17–5:17; Titus 2:11–14: What specific behaviors, attitudes, thought patterns, or other things are hindering you from becoming a person who is zealous for good deeds and who leads a sensible, righteous, and godly life in this present age?

Colossians 3:1–4, 16–17, 23–24: What specific things must *you* do in order to "keep seeking the things above"? What specific things must you refrain from doing? How do these activities affect your daily, routine activities of life?

3. Develop a *personal prayer plan* using the "journalism questions" found in this lesson. This plan should be broad enough and flexible enough to use in different types of prayer situations, but specific enough to keep you focused on God and His purposes in all those different types of situations.

Digging Deeper

1. Explain how carefully planning your prayer life could actually enhance its spontaneity, enthusiasm, interest, and appeal.

2. Carefully read Jeremiah 7–14 along with 1 John 5 and explain why God instructs us *not* to pray for certain people described in those passages. What insight into the nature of God do these passages give you?

5

The Priority of Worship

Remember, O my soul,
It is thy duty and privilege to rejoice in God:
He requires it of thee for all his favours of grace.
Rejoice then in the giver and his goodness,
Be happy in him, O my heart, and in nothing but God,
  for whatever a man trusts in,
  from that he expects happiness.
He who is the ground of thy faith
  should be the substance of thy joy.
  —From *The Valley of Vision:*
    A Collection of Puritan Prayers
    and Devotions

Since its publication in 1961, A. W. Tozer's brief but powerful book *The Knowledge of the Holy* has become a classic on worship. Every time I return to my well-worn copy, I am struck by these words from his opening chapter:

> What comes into our minds when we think about God is the most important thing about us.

49

The history of mankind will probably show that no people has ever risen above its religion, and man's spiritual history will positively demonstrate that no religion has ever been greater than its idea of God. Worship is pure or base as the worshiper entertains high or low thoughts of God. . . .

That our idea of God correspond as nearly as possible to the true being of God is of immense importance to us. . . . I believe there is scarcely an error in doctrine or a failure in applying Christian ethics that cannot be traced finally to imperfect and ignoble thoughts about God.[1]

Although Tozer was not specifically addressing the topic of prayer, everything that he said relates to it directly. Worship resides at the heart of all genuine prayer. Thus, if we don't worship well, we won't pray well either. When you and I pray, we seek to commune with our Father God. Communing with Him requires knowing Him well; and knowing Him well compels us to worship.

When God places us in His family, He gives us a hunger to understand Him and love Him. Then He invites us to feast on the nourishing truths about Him that are found in the Bible. As we partake from this lavish table, we experience something very unusual. Our hunger for God is *intensified* in the process of being satisfied. Strange as it may seem, the more we know about God, the *more* we long to know *more*. One natural response to this longing is worshipful prayer; and such prayer, in turn, produces obedient service.

R. C. Sproul echoes Tozer's rich insights when he says, "How we understand the person and character of God the Father affects every aspect of our lives."[2] We can only walk worthy of our high calling in Christ if we think about God as He really is. The truth about God is found in the Scriptures; therefore, our worship, our prayers, and our service depend on how well we digest God's revealed truth.

Yielding to the temptation to gorge ourselves on the junk food of the world will not satisfy our hunger for God, but it can dull it. When our desire to know God is thus dimmed, we will be less prone to worship. That waning worship will cripple our prayers. And as the effectiveness of prayer fades, so does our service.

As we work through this lesson together, let's concentrate on how prayer that is anchored in Scripture satisfies and intensifies our hunger for a true knowledge of God, which equips us for service as it compels us to worship.

The Church's Highest Priority

Even though worship is central to our life in God's family, it tends to be overshadowed by more "active" pursuits. Ask a group of Christians, "What is the first priority of the church?" and most will respond, "Evangelism." Some will say, "Fellowship." A few will tell you it is "teaching and equipping the saints." But, amazingly, almost none will say "worship."

Jesus told the Samaritan woman at the well that God *seeks true worshippers* (John 4:23). He knew that only true worshippers would become effective evangelists, teachers, and fellowship-coordinators. Each of those ministries is essential to the work of the church, and doing each of them well depends on how well we worship.

We Christians tend to elevate "active" work above worship because it is much easier. It can be outlined, accomplished, and evaluated. It satisfies our desire to be useful, productive, and needed. It gives us a sense of worth and identity, as well as a ready response to the oft-asked question, "What do you do?" God designed us as workers (Genesis 2:15) and chastises the lazy (2 Thessalonians 3:10–15).

But He demands that our work glorify Him, not ourselves (Colossians 3:23). Grounding our work in true worship is the only way we can do that.

Worship is harder than work because it requires us to set self aside and marvel at God. Worship demands fascination with God's attributes, wonder at His works, fear of His power, and amazement in His presence. It calls us to "be still" and know that He is God (Psalm 46:10 NKJV). We find true worship so hard because we don't like being still, and we're simply too busy to know God very well. Perhaps that is why He designed prayer as a method of worship. Prayer calls us away from our busyness to learn stillness so that we can get to know God.

Learning Stillness Through Prayer

Stillness cuts cross-grain to our culture. We are a people addicted to noise and frenzied activity. We have little desire and even less opportunity to remain quietly immobile for long periods of time. If we are to obey God's command to be still, we must first learn how to do it. Open-Book prayer helps us learn stillness as we set aside noise and activity to hear God speak truth through His Word. Psalm 131 captures the essence of stillness that will help us to listen:

> O LORD, my heart is not proud, nor my eyes
> haughty;
> Nor do I involve myself in great matters,
> Or in things too difficult for me.
> Surely I have composed and quieted my soul;
> Like a weaned child rests against his mother,
> My soul is like a weaned child within me.
> O Israel, hope in the LORD
> From this time forth and forever.

The stillness to which God calls us in Scripture consists in trust and dependence as opposed to self-reliance and self-importance. Jesus described true worshippers for the Samaritan woman as those who worship God "in spirit and truth" (John 4:24). In other words, worship is a spiritual activity conducted according to divine revelation. It presupposes a spiritual connection between a redeemed soul and its Redeemer, as well as a heart-mind-will inclined toward obedience.

Only those who have been redeemed and transformed through the miracle of salvation have the spiritual connection with God needed for the stillness of worship. We know that our relationship with Him is based on Christ's work, not our own, and that "He who did not spare His own Son, but delivered Him up for us all" (Romans 8:32) can be trusted to give us freely every good thing we need. As we learn to define our needs through His Word (see lessons 4 and 9), we come to appreciate more fully both His perfect provision and our complete dependence on Him.

Open-Book prayer isn't noisy or frenzied. It quietly listens to God's gracious assurances of His love, care, and pardon. And it short-circuits our attempts to move Him through self-righteous eloquence, ego-inflated demands, or worldly-wise bargaining. It helps us curb pride and quiet our souls so that we can rest hopefully and wholly in His great sufficiency. Open-Book prayer does, indeed, foster the stillness we need to get to know God.

Knowing He Is God

Worship demands stillness because we can't worship a God we don't know. And knowledge of God comes solely through His revelation of Himself in nature, the Scriptures, and His Son, Jesus Christ.

Basic knowledge of God comes to everyone through creation. Romans 1:20–21 says, "Since the creation of the world His invisible attributes, His eternal power and divine nature, have been clearly seen, being understood through what has been made, so that they are without excuse. For even though they knew God, they did not honor Him as God, or give thanks."

Natural revelation is, therefore, sufficient to acquaint sinful men and women with God's existence, power, and wisdom. It is sufficient to establish their responsibility to honor God, thank Him, and give Him glory. But it is not sufficient to save them from His righteous wrath. Saving knowledge of God must come from the written revelation of Scripture.[3] Only here do we find "the wisdom that leads to salvation" as well as the teaching, reproof, correction, and training that equip us for service (2 Timothy 3:15–17).

As we pursue the stillness of open-Book prayer, we become better acquainted with our heavenly Father. What we learn in the Bible about Him drives us to worship. God reveals Himself to us as the Creator (Genesis 1–2), who fills heaven and earth (Jeremiah 23:24); as the Lord God of hosts (Romans 9:29), who is present and near (Psalm 139:7); and as the God who provides (Genesis 22:14), heals (Deuteronomy 32:39), and sanctifies (Exodus 31:13). Moreover, He offers Himself as our banner (Exodus 17:15), our peace (Hebrews 13:20), and our shepherd (Psalm 23).

The Psalms describe God as "great . . . above all gods" (135:5) in whom no evil dwells (5:4). They say He is "resplendent" (76:4), righteous (71:19), strong (68:34), awesome (65:5), holy, and great (77:13). They tell us He is "compassionate and gracious, slow to anger and abounding in lovingkindness" (103:8), "clothed in splendor and majesty, covering [Him]self with light as with a cloak" (104:1–2). On a more personal note, they own Him as "my strength and song . . . [who] has become my salvation"

(118:14), "my stronghold" (62:2), "a shield about me, My glory, and the One who lifts my head" (3:3), "my hope [and] . . . confidence" (71:5), and "our refuge and strength, a very present help in trouble" (46:1).

God reveals even more of Himself as He allows us to listen while He demands of a petulant Job, "Where were you when I laid the foundation of the earth!" (Job 38:4); or declares to an awe-filled Moses, "No man can see Me and live!" (Exodus 33:20); or reminds King Asa, "The eyes of the LORD move to and fro throughout the earth that He may strongly support those whose heart is completely His" (2 Chronicles 16:9).

The prophet Isaiah exclaims,

> To whom then will you liken God?
> Or what likeness will you compare with Him? . . .
> Do you not know? Have you not heard?
> The Everlasting God, the LORD, the Creator of the
>   ends of the earth
> Does not become weary or tired.
> His understanding is inscrutable.
> He gives strength to the weary,
> And to him who lacks might He increases power.
>   (40:18, 28–29)

And Jeremiah proclaims,

> There is none like Thee, O LORD;
> Thou art great, and great is Thy name in
>   might. . . .
> But the LORD is the true God;
> He is the living God and the everlasting King.
> At His wrath the earth quakes,
> And the nations cannot endure His indignation.
>   (10:6, 10)

It's hard to imagine how any transformed saint of God could remain unmoved to worship in the face of such glorious divine declarations!

Open-Book prayer helps us think about God as He really is. These thoughts then compel us to give worship the highest priority. That, in turn, makes our prayers effective. Concentrating on God's character and works as we pray bends our hearts to His will as it reinforces thanksgiving, stimulates repentance, and molds supplication.

Notes

1. A. W. Tozer, *The Knowledge of the Holy* (San Francisco: Harper and Row, 1961), vii.

2. R. C. Sproul, *The Holiness of God* (Wheaton, Ill.: Tyndale House, 1985, 1998), 25.

3. Bear in mind that God's revelation of Himself in the Incarnation of Christ is contained in and inseparable from the written revelation of Scripture.

Exercises

Review

1. Read and think about the short prayer taken from *The Valley of Vision,* which introduces this lesson. Then explain any connection you see between it and the material contained in the lesson. (This is a personal, highly subjective question and thus does not have one *right* answer.)

2. In your own words, describe how A. W. Tozer's thoughts on worship (pp. 49–50) relate directly to prayer.

3. What is the first priority of the church? Support your answer with Scripture.

4. Discuss the importance of "stillness" to worship. Then describe how open-Book prayer encourages stillness.

5. Describe a "true worshipper." Then describe how a true worshipper prays.

6. List several characteristics and works of God discussed in this lesson. Then explain how concentrating on them can make your prayers more effective.

Application

1. *Open-Book Prayer:* During your prayer time for the following month, meditate on five different Psalms per day to help you be still and worship God in spirit and truth. If the next month contains thirty-one days, feel free to devote one day solely to Psalm 119.

2. Compile a list of the topics you normally cover in prayer. Concentrate on being complete and specific. (Your list should contain a minimum of fifteen to twenty items.) Now categorize your list. Next to each item, place an "A" for adoration, a "C" for confession, or an "S" for supplication. Then examine the wording of the items. Are they expressed in language that reflects a grateful heart? Does your list indicate that *worship* is the first priority of your prayers? Explain your answer. If worship does not seem to be the highest priority in your prayers, pay particular attention to Application 1.

3. As you meditate on five different Psalms this week, analyze and record how this focus on worship enhances

your gratitude, stimulates you to confess your sin, and re-aligns your requests. Give specific examples to support your analysis.

Digging Deeper

1. Research from Scripture and reliable biblical reference tools, the following names of God, and then explain how addressing God by these names (or their English equivalents) in your prayers could help you worship Him more meaningfully and thus pray more effectively:

Elohim

Jehovah-Nissi

Jehovah-Raah

Jehovah-Shama

El Elyon

Jehovah-Rapha

Jehovah-Tsidkenu

Jehovah-Magodeshkim

Jehovah-Jireh

Jehovah-Shalom

Jehovah-Sabaoth

6

The Power of the Name

Christ does not assure us that all of our requests will be granted if we repeat a formula. Instead, He teaches that those requests which are in accordance with His Name—that is, His holy character as our intercessor—will be granted by the Father. —Richard L. Pratt, Jr.

The adult Sunday school teacher at my church opened our study one morning by asking, "What is the most important question in the world?" After a few moments of silence, a woman in the back responded, "I would say, 'Do you know Jesus?' "

"That's an extremely important question," the teacher assured her. "But I can think of one that's even more important. Any other ideas?" More silence ensued. Finally a quiet voice on the front row suggested, "How about, 'Who is Jesus?' "

"Exactly!" Our teacher's eyes lit up. "Do you see why that question is more important than the first one? Asking if someone knows Jesus takes on critical importance *only* if

Jesus is worth knowing. And the only way to find out if He's worth knowing is to investigate who He is."

Our discussion that morning certainly whetted our appetites for the new quarter. For the next thirteen weeks we used Joseph Pipa's outstanding book *The Root and Branch* to guide us through a scriptural investigation of who Jesus is. And by the time we were finished, I not only had gained a deeper love for my Savior, but also understood much more clearly how His work of redemption relates to prayer "in His name."

Magic or Miracle

On the eve of His crucifixion, Jesus gathered His disciples for their last meal together. He used that precious time to remind them of the truths that would sustain them during the dark days ahead. The scriptural account of that Passover reminder, known as the Upper Room Discourse, contains some of His most beloved teaching. It is laced with astounding, confidence-building promises, three of which relate to prayer "in His name."

> And whatever you ask in My name, that will I do, that the Father may be glorified in the Son. If you ask Me anything in My name, I will do it. (John 14:13–14)

> You did not choose Me, but I chose you, and appointed you, that you should go and bear fruit, and that your fruit should remain, that whatever you ask of the Father in My name, He may give to you." (15:16)

> Truly, truly, I say to you, if you shall ask the Father for anything, He will give it to you in My name.

Until now you have asked for nothing in My name;
ask, and you will receive, that your joy may be
made full. (16:23–24)

If you read those verses quickly because you've read them
before, please go back and read them again slowly and carefully. Pretend you are one of the men in that room hearing
them for the very first time. What amazing statements! Three
iron-clad promises piled one on the other guaranteeing success for prayers directed to God "in Jesus' name." The Savior was promising His disciples great power wrapped up in
three little words. But exactly what kind of power did those
words contain? Was it magical—or miraculous?

Defining the power contained in those words requires
understanding the context in which they are found. The
Upper Room Discourse was delivered to history's most significant leadership team—eleven men who stood on the
brink of a crisis of which they were only vaguely aware.
Their leader had been given the task of preparing them for
what could be described as the world's most fiercely opposed takeover. He would be returning to heaven and leaving *them* to establish God's kingdom on earth. He had spent
three years preparing them and was leaving them well
equipped for their mission. As His time of departure neared,
He had to make sure they could *use* what He'd given them.

Aside from His indwelling Spirit and the Old Testament
Scriptures, their most valuable resource would be prayer.
Making their requests known to the Father *in the name of
the Son* was the means God had ordained of supplying their
needs in His service "according to His riches in glory"
(Philippians 4:6, 19). However, the phrase, "in Jesus' name"
was no magical incantation. It spoke of the miraculous
union with Christ they had received through salvation.[1] No
longer dead in trespasses and sins, no longer by nature
children of wrath (Ephesians 2:1, 3), they had been justi-

fied, redeemed, and transformed through the work of Christ Jesus. Now holy and blameless in the dress of Christ's righteousness, they had privileged access to the Father's overflowing storehouse of blessing through the name of the Son.

The Conditions of Power

The prayer promises Jesus made to His disciples on the eve of His death were undeniably "iron-clad," but *not* unconditional. (If you thought they were, read them again!) The power of prayer in His name is reserved—by three key conditions—for those chosen by God to show forth His glory (Isaiah 43:7) by seeking His kingdom as their highest priority and greatest delight (Matthew 6:33).

The first promise (John 14:13–14) places a condition on prayer by describing it as an instrument by which God glorifies Himself. The second (John 15:16) does so by declaring that prayer in God's name is for those who have been chosen and appointed to bear lasting fruit. And the third (John 16:23–24) affirms that such prayer "fills up" the joy of those whom God has so chosen.

Thus, we see from the Savior's own words that the power inherent in His glorious name does not derive from the mere act of invoking it. Rather, it proceeds from our redemptive union with Him, which transforms us and realigns our purposes with His (John 15:1–7). Prayer in His name becomes prayer in harmony with the desires of the Savior to whom we've been joined. We might just as well close our prayers with the words, "I ask these things because I believe that Jesus would request them in this situation."

Righteous Standing Before God

The three conditions that characterize prayer in Jesus' name were exemplified in His own life as the first-born among many brethren and our sympathetic High Priest. Scripture tells us that He glorified God on earth by accomplishing all the work He had been given to do (John 17:4). Jesus did this both in joy (John 15:11) and for the joy set before Him (Hebrews 12:2). Our union with Him in salvation, however, provides us with much more than an *example* to follow in our lives and prayers. It also did something amazing for us, something we could not begin to do for ourselves.

Jesus actually lived, in complete obedience to God's law, the perfectly righteous life required of us all. Since the Fall, the curse of sin has prevented any of us from living out that requirement. Therefore, we were barred from the presence of a Holy God who is "of purer eyes than to behold evil, and cannot look on wickedness" (Habakkuk 1:13 NKJV). But when salvation placed us in union with Christ, His righteousness was credited to us, giving us access to the Father *in the name of the Son*.

Thus, when we pray in the name of our Savior, we not only consciously harmonize our requests with His purposes; we also acknowledge our complete dependence upon His righteousness for the privilege of approaching God's throne.

Fulfilling Our Chief End

The privilege of praying in Jesus' name should be cherished by all Christians. It is a blessed means of fulfilling our "chief end" of glorifying and enjoying God (Westminster Shorter Catechism, Q/A 1) as we pursue the good works for which we were created *in Christ Jesus* (Ephesians 2:10). Framing our prayers in His name reminds us of our transformed standing in Christ and helps us "set our minds on things above, not on the things that are on earth" (Colossians 3:2).

Establishing prayer as a worshipful priority and defining our needs according to Scripture reminds us that God is both able and willing to equip us fully for our every good work in His service. Prayer in the name of the Son turns our sphere of influence into a magnificent gallery for displaying God's glory. Those around us observe God at work in the world when they see Him fill up our joy by perfectly meeting each need we bring to Him in prayer.

God's work in the lives of those who pray in His Son's name thus becomes a "sweet aroma of the knowledge of Him in every place. . . . to the one an aroma from death to death, to the other an aroma from life to life" (2 Corinthians 2:14, 16). Prayer in Jesus' name is far from a magical formula used to bend God to our purposes. It reflects instead the reality of our redeemed standing in Christ and, in so doing, exalts God by displaying the amazing work of His grace before the eyes of the world.

Notes

1. For an insightful discussion of our union with Christ in salvation see John Murray's excellent book, *Redemption Accomplished and Applied* (Grand Rapids: Eerdmans, 1955).

Exercises

Review

1. What do *you* think is the most important question in the world? Support your answer with Scripture.

2. Describe the conditions associated with Jesus' great promises regarding prayer in His name.

3. How does our standing in Christ affect the privilege of prayer?

4. Describe the way praying in Jesus' name enhances our ability to fulfill the chief end for which we were created.

5. Explain the connection between praying in Jesus' name and what you learned in lesson 4 about defining your needs according to Scripture as well as what you learned in lesson 5 about the priority of worship in prayer.

6. Based on what you have learned in this lesson and on your understanding of Scripture in general, explain Richard Pratt's statement, ". . . those requests which are in accordance with His Name—that is, His holy character as our intercessor—will be granted by the Father."

Application

1. *Open-Book Prayer:* In your prayer time this week, use John 14:13–14; 15:15; and 16:23–24 to remind yourself:

   (a) to make only those requests the answers to which would bring glory to God,

   (b) that your prayers should reflect that you have been chosen and appointed by God to bear lasting fruit, and

   (c) that God's answering of your prayers should be a primary source of your joy.

2. Consider your recent prayer requests, and explain how they would change if you replaced the phrase, "In Jesus' name, amen," with "I believe these are the things Jesus would prayer for in this situation." Give specific examples of how your requests would change.

Digging Deeper

1. If you are familiar with the current "Lordship Controversy" within the evangelical church, consider the issues involved in this controversy in light of what you have learned in this lesson regarding prayer in Jesus' name. That is, since praying in Jesus' name flows from our *union* with Christ in salvation, which turns our hearts toward aligning our purposes with His, how effectively would a person who regards Jesus as Savior but not as Lord be able to pray "in His name"? If you are not familiar with this controversy, use this question as an incentive to acquaint yourself with the issues. (In your research, be sure to include a study of Michael Horton's book, *Christ the Lord*.)

2. Read John Murray's book *Redemption Accomplished and Applied* and summarize the key points he makes about our union with Christ. Then explain how your understanding of your union with Christ in salvation relates to prayer "in His name."

LESSON 7

The Role of
the Spirit

*When the Spirit works by the Word, He makes it effec-
tual, through His operations, to build up and perfect the
saint.* —A. W. Pink

About an hour ago, I hit the "delete" key on my trusty Mac-
intosh, wiped out two days' work on this lesson, and went
for a walk. I walk when I'm frustrated, discouraged, or angry.
After jettisoning almost four pages of text, I was all three. The
task of describing how God's Holy Spirit works in our lives
has never been easy for me. And my two-day struggle to de-
pict His role in our prayers had proved distressingly fruitless.

I fumed for six blocks and then found myself chuckling.
The very same Spirit I was having so much trouble describing had patiently waited for the first break in my fuss-
ing and then quietly dropped Romans 8:26–27 into my dis-
gruntled thoughts.

> In the same way the Spirit also helps our weakness;
> for we do not know how to pray as we should, but

the Spirit Himself intercedes for us with groanings too deep for words; and He who searches the hearts knows what the mind of the Spirit is, because He intercedes for the saints according to the will of God.

I had been "nudged" to stop fuming and start asking for help. "Lord God," I prayed silently (for when I pray aloud, my neighbors give me strange looks). "Thank you for giving me your indwelling Spirit to help me. I don't know why I have so much trouble articulating His work, but I do know that You want me to write about His role in our prayers. I confess my frustration, discouragement, and anger at not being able to express the very things I am now experiencing! And I am asking your Spirit to help me pray even as I seek a way to describe His role in prayer."

The Spirit Works Through the Word

As I rounded the park at the edge of my neighborhood, my agitation began to subside. Calmness and peace settled over my spirit and soon freed my mind to pursue clearer thinking. *Obviously, God's Spirit is helping me pray,* I thought. *But just how is He doing it?*

Then it hit me: *He helped you to pray by bringing Scripture to mind.*

Of course! The Spirit works through the Word. I knew that principle well. I had taught it and written about it. But I had neglected to apply it to the Spirit's work in our prayers. No wonder I was struggling.

I hurried back to my desk to renew my acquaintance with the two parallel passages of Scripture that best demonstrate (at least in my mind) this key characteristic of the Spirit's work. If you haven't read Ephesians 5:18–6:19 alongside Colossians 3:16–4:6 recently, please take a moment to do so before going on with this lesson.

Were you able to pick out the fundamental relationship between the Word and the Spirit in those verses? In Ephesians 5:18 Paul says, "Be filled[1] with the Spirit," and then launches into a discussion of the glorious results of heeding that counsel. Being filled with the Spirit inevitably fills us with joy—the kind of joy that makes music and melody (v. 19). Being filled with the Spirit instills within us an attitude of thanksgiving toward God (v. 20) and humility toward others (v. 21).

It helps us order our family, work, and community relationships in ways that honor God by reflecting His attributes (5:22–6:9). It gives us the strength we need in the Lord to wage war against the spiritual forces of wickedness in the heavenly places (6:10–17). And last but certainly not least, praying "at all times *in the Spirit*" keeps us alert to petition God in behalf of the saints, particularly those called to "make known with boldness the mystery of the gospel" (vv. 18–19).

All these benefits are the work of the *Spirit* in Ephesians 5:18–6:19. But when we turn to Colossians 3:16–4:6, we find something different—and yet amazingly the same.

In Colossians 3:16, Paul says "Let the *word* of Christ richly dwell within you." But then he describes *the very same results we saw in Ephesians!* Do you see what he's done? In the process of recording inspired, inerrant, infallible Scripture, the apostle Paul *identified* the work of the indwelling Spirit with the work of the indwelling Word.

As I pondered the great foundational truth contained in these passages, I realized I had hit on the secret of what I had been calling "open-Book prayer." Now I knew why my own prayer life had been so profoundly transformed by my pastor's dedication to teaching us to pray directly from Scripture. And I also knew why my primary aim in writing this book (along with glorifying God) is to extend that profound impact to your prayer life as well.

Light for Your Prayers

The God-honoring, ministry-energizing, holiness-inspiring power of open-Book prayer lies in the work of God's indwelling Spirit called *illumination.* You may recall from previous studies that God's truth comes to us through three essential processes: revelation, inspiration, and illumination.[2] Revelation involves the actual disclosure of God's truth; inspiration has to do with recording divine revelation perfectly and completely; and illumination is what enables us to understand that truth.

Without this illuminating work of the Holy Spirit within us, we could not understand Scripture. Paul tells us in 1 Corinthians 2 that the Bible contains "God's wisdom" (v. 7), which "none of the rulers of this age has understood" (v. 8). They do not understand it because "a natural man does not accept the things of the Spirit of God; for they are foolishness to him, and he cannot understand them, because they are spiritually appraised" (v. 14).

Christians, however, "have received, not the spirit of the world, but the Spirit who is from God, that we might know the things freely given to us by God" (v. 12). It is the gracious gift of God's indwelling Spirit that enables His children to understand Scripture. But we should be grateful that His work doesn't stop there. In Galatians 5, Paul informs us that the Spirit also helps us *live* in keeping with the truth He has brought to light in our minds: "Walk by the Spirit, and you will not carry out the desires of the flesh" (v. 16). Rather, you will manifest the "fruit of the Spirit" which is "love, joy, peace, patience, kindness, goodness, faithfulness, gentleness, [and] self-control" (vv. 22–23).

The more we yield ourselves to the equipping work of the Spirit, the more His fruit will flourish in our behavior and attitudes. Our lives will be enriched by the benefits described in the parallel passages from Ephesians and Colossians mentioned above. Among those benefits is effective, powerful prayer.

How Does He Do It?

We have seen that the Spirit helps us to pray by His work through the Word. But if you're anything like me, broad principles like that remain frustratingly hazy unless clarified by a few examples. So, let's sharpen our focus by examining some of the ways the Spirit works through the Word to help us pray.

The Spirit helps us to pray by validating our privilege. Since Christians alone may claim the family privilege of prayer (see lesson 2), the Holy Spirit's work of *assuring* us of our redemption helps us to pray. The eighth chapter of Romans describes how the Spirit validates our personal privilege of approaching God's throne.

Those who are in Christ Jesus will not be condemned, we read in verse 1, because "the law of the Spirit of life in Christ Jesus has set [them] free from the law of sin and death" (v. 2). God Himself condemned sin in the flesh by sending His Son as an offering for sin (v. 3). He also fulfilled the requirements of His law in His elect by applying Christ's righteousness to them (v. 4).

Those who "do not walk according to the flesh, but according to the Spirit" can be confident that they belong to God's family because their minds are set on the things of the Spirit rather than the things of the flesh (vv. 4–5). The unredeemed cannot set their minds on the things of the Spirit because they are by nature hostile to God and cannot please Him (v. 6–8).

All Christians have the Holy Spirit living within them (v. 9). We are assured of His presence both by His leading (v. 14) and by His personal witness to our spirits that we are children of God (v. 16). As the Spirit leads us in righteousness by illuminating our understanding of Scripture and enabling us to apply it, and as He testifies personally of His indwelling presence, we gain assurance of our redemption and of our privilege of prayer.

The Spirit helps us to pray by making Christ known and glorifying Him. The life of Christ is the fullest revelation of God to humanity. Jesus told His disciples on the eve of His death, "He who has seen Me has seen the Father" (John 14:9). Other New Testament Scriptures describe Him as "the image of the invisible God" (Colossians 1:15) and "the radiance of His glory and the exact representation of His nature" (Hebrews 1:3).

God's plan of salvation was accomplished through the work of the Son and applied to us by the Spirit. As we have seen, an essential part of the Spirit's work is His illumination of Scripture to our minds. Without that, we would have no capacity to understand spiritual truth or glorify God.

In His Upper Room Discourse, Jesus foretold of this ministry of the Spirit:

> When He, the Spirit of truth, comes, He will guide you into all the truth; for He will not speak on His own initiative, but whatever He hears, He will speak; and He will disclose to you what is to come. He shall glorify Me; for He shall take of Mine, and shall disclose it to you. All things that the Father has are Mine; therefore I said, that He takes of Mine, and will disclose it to you. (John 16:13–15)

By magnifying the person and work of Christ, the Holy Spirit prompts our hearts to respond in prayerful praise and thanksgiving.

The Spirit helps us to pray by convicting us of our sin and assuring us of forgiveness. Although our salvation in Christ is eternally secured by an irrevocable transaction known as justification, the harmony of our daily walk with God by which we glorify and enjoy Him is often disrupted by sin. When it is, the Holy Spirit works through God's Word to convict us of that sin and prompt us to ask forgiveness.

The Spirit wields the sharp, two-edged sword of God's Word so that it pierces the deepest recesses of our being, judging the thoughts and intentions of our hearts (Hebrews 4:12). Against God's high standard of righteousness for His children (see Ephesians 4:1–3, 17–5:14), we stand convicted of sin and in need of cleansing forgiveness.

That forgiveness is never more than a sincere prayer away. The Spirit uses the Word not only to convict but also to promise forgiveness (see 1 John 1:9). He thereby imbues us with confidence to approach the throne of grace boldly to receive His grace and mercy (Hebrews 4:15–16).

The Spirit helps us to pray by shaping our perception of needs. In lesson 4, we briefly discussed the role of open-Book prayer in helping us distinguish between worldly desires and our legitimate needs in God's service. In lesson 9 we will discuss this topic in greater detail. For now, let me simply point out that without the illuminating work of God's indwelling Spirit, we would not be able to understand the truths of Scripture that define the needs we should present to God in our prayers.

The Spirit helps us to pray by assuring us of His direct intercession. The Spirit also works through the Word to assist our prayers by assuring us of His *direct* intercession with God for us when we are most helpless. I am sure this is what He was doing when I had reached my wit's end with this lesson and fled my house for a walk. With a reminder of the great truth contained in Romans 8:26–27, He replaced my agitation with assurance of His direct intercession in my time of weakness.

My inability to articulate a great truth of God was an intellectual weakness to which I had responded in spiritual weakness by sinning. My frustration, discouragement, and anger reflected my unbelief that God could and would enable me to finish the task He had given me. By using His Word to remind me of His indwelling presence, the Spirit convicted me of my sin and prompted my prayer of confession.

By the same action, He comforted me with the assurance that He was praying for me in complete accord with God's will even when I was too weak to know how to pray for myself. He interceded for me through a form of inter-Trinitarian communication described as "groanings too deep for words"—which although decidedly mysterious, is undeniably effective.

I have written the lesson I could not write, and there is only one explanation: God's indwelling Spirit prays for us in our weakness and works through the Word to equip us for His service.

Notes

1. "Be filled" translates the Greek word *plēroō* and would be more literally rendered "be being kept filled." It is used here as a command demanding conscious, continual action on our part. Therefore, this verse refers to our ongoing responsibility to yield our attitudes, thoughts, and actions to the control of the indwelling Holy Spirit rather than to the initial indwelling of the Spirit that occurs at salvation. Ephesians 5:18 is, therefore, a sanctification verse, not a salvation verse.

2. See lesson 3 of the Light for Your Path study, *A Book Like No Other,* for an in-depth discussion of these three processes.

Exercises

Review

1. Describe the connection between God's Word and His Spirit found in Ephesians 5:18–6:19 and Colossians 3:16–4:6.

2. Why can the Holy Spirit's work of illumination be seen as the "secret" of open-Book prayer?

3. Explain how the Spirit helps us to pray by validating our privilege.

4. Explain how the Spirit helps us to pray by teaching us about God and about what God has done.

5. How does the Spirit's work of conviction help us to pray?

6. How does the Spirit's intercession for us with groanings too deep for words benefit us?

Application

1. *Open-Book Prayer:* In your prayer time this week, use Romans 8 to help you focus on and appreciate the Spirit's work of assurance and intercession as you pray.

2. Describe a time in your Christian life when weakness prevented you from knowing how to pray as you should.

In your description, explain the weakness itself and your response to it. How did the Holy Spirit help you? In answering this question, consider the following: What Scriptures did He bring to your mind? Did these Scriptures assure you of your privileged standing before God as His child? Did they teach you about God's great attributes and work? Did they convict you of sin and assure you of forgiveness? Did they help you clarify the difference between worldly desire and genuine need in God's service? Did they assure you of the Spirit's direct intercession with God on your behalf? Did they help you in some other way? If so, explain. Now describe the outcome of the Spirit's helping you in this weakness. What have you learned about prayer from this circumstance?

Digging Deeper

1. Describe one or more abuses of prayer of which you are aware. Then explain how an understanding of how the Spirit works through the Word would prevent or correct each abuse. Support your explanation with specific scriptural references relevant to each abuse.

8

Prayer and Stiff Kids

When our Lord and Master Jesus Christ said, "Repent"
(Matthew 4:17), He willed that the whole life of believ-
ers should be one of repentance.
                    —The First of Luther's Ninety-Five Theses

In his book *Approaching God,* Steve Brown recalls the day
a member of his congregation dropped by his office to
share a profound truth she was sure he could use in a book
or sermon. "Pastor," she said solemnly. "It is very difficult
to hug a stiff kid."[1] Obviously, that woman knew her pastor's work well. Brown's adroit use of such powerful word
pictures ranks him among Christianity's most effective
communicators. If you've read any of his books, you know
what I mean. The colorful hues in which he paints truth
make it very hard to forget.

Brown did use her shared truth in his insightful book
about prayer. In so doing, he seared into my mind an in-
delible image of our loving Father seeking—at times with
infinite patience and persistence—to hug *His* stiff kids.

What Makes a Kid Stiff?

Have *you* ever tried to hug a stiff kid? I have and I can tell you it's no easy task. Stiff kids aren't responsive. And a lack of response invariably kills a good hug. In much the same way, unresponsiveness on the part of God's kids greatly hinders their prayer lives and disrupts the fellowship with God that prayer is intended to foster.

We saw in our last lesson that one of the ways the Holy Spirit functions in prayer is by convicting us of the sin that plagues us as Christians. Such sin cannot *destroy* our family relationship with God; that relationship has been secured by Jesus' death for us (Romans 8:1; 35–39). But sin does *disrupt the harmony* of our walk with Him.

Our God is holy and righteous, and has chosen each of His children to live in a close, personal relationship with Him—one that brings Him glory and fills us with joy. But that raises a question. How can a God whose eyes are too pure to look upon evil (Habakkuk 1:13) enter into fellowship with fallen sinners? The answer is, through a substitutionary process called *imputation*.

Second Corinthians 5:21 presents salvation as a great exchange in which God "made Him who knew no sin to be sin on our behalf, that we might become the righteousness of God in Him." But God's graciousness toward us doesn't stop there. Not only does He "legally" impute (or ascribe) Christ's righteous record to us so that we can enter His presence, but He also works through His Spirit to conform our actual behavior to the image of Christ. This He does through another process called *sanctification* (2 Corinthians 3:18). If you have ever heard people describe the Christian life as "a process of becoming what we already are in Christ Jesus," this is the theological truth they are describing.

Prayer plays an important role in that growing process. But stiffness on our part interferes with our prayers and thus hampers our sanctification. When the Holy Spirit convicts us of sin, our "natural" reaction is to stiffen in guilt. When this happens, Steve Brown reminds us, we can't blame the *sin* for crippling our prayer lives; it's our own stubborn resistance to the Spirit's conviction that creates static in our communication with God.[2]

Sin, Up Close and Personal

If you and I are to walk worthy of our high calling in Christ (Ephesians 4:1), we simply cannot follow the current trend in the church toward downplaying sin. We must resist those who tell us to eliminate sin from our presentations of the gospel and to focus instead on how Jesus stands ready to meet every felt need. We must refuse to redesign God, according to our own preferences, into someone without an ounce of holy wrath in His being. And we must remind ourselves daily to take up the cross upon which we have been commanded to crucify self in order to follow Him.

We cannot *be* Christians and ignore the doctrine of sin. Satisfaction of God's righteous wrath against sin lies at the very core of the gospel. And it is through the Christian's ongoing battle with sin that God has chosen to glorify Himself in the world. Thus, confession of sin in our prayers is essential to both our initial redemption and our ongoing sanctification.

In the book of Acts, the apostles who ignited the spreading flame of the church were often asked, "What must we do to be saved?" Their answers invariably emphasized *repentance from sin* (Acts 2:38–39; 3:18–19; 26:20). "Repentance" has to do with a change of mind, as well as a change of direction. When people repent, they change their minds about God and change their behavior accordingly (1 Thessalonians 1:9).

Salvation occurs when the Holy Spirit opens people's

hearts to believe what the Bible says (Acts 16:14), convicts them regarding the sin separating them from God (Isaiah 59:2), and moves them to turn from sin and serve the Lord with gladness (Acts 3:19; 1 Thessalonians 1:9). Prayer is the means by which new converts express and submit to these great truths.

People new in the faith quickly discover that although their redemption delivered them from the penalty of sin, it did not inoculate them against its allure. Yet, as they seek wisdom in Scripture (James 1:5), they learn of God's purposes for leaving them vulnerable. Second Corinthians 4:7 assures us that "we have this treasure in earthen vessels, that the surpassing greatness of the power may be of God and not from ourselves."

The treasure referred to in this verse is the truth of the gospel. That truth not only proclaims deliverance of the elect from condemnation (Romans 8:1) but also enables them to glorify God by overcoming temptation in the power of the Spirit (1 John 4:4).[3] If God had not left us susceptible to the enticement of sin, we would have lost this unique privilege of reflecting His glory.

Salvation not only rescues us from God's righteous judgment and empowers us in His service; it also transforms us into people who *appreciate* our deliverance and *desire* to obey Him (Ezekiel 11:19–20; 36:26–27). That is why the apostle John describes genuine Christians as those who have come to know Him and keep His commandments (1 John 2:3–5). True believers are recognizable because their lives are not *characterized* by sin (3:5–8), even though they do *commit* sins (1:8). When they do commit sins, the Spirit convicts their now-tender hearts (Ezekiel 11:19–20; 36:26–27) to sense their true guilt.

No one likes to feel guilty—and with good reason. God built discomfort into feelings of guilt to encourage repentance. When we respond by confessing our sin in prayer and seeking His forgiveness (1 John 1:9), we provide God one more opportunity to display His glory to the world through His dealings with us. But when we stiffen in un-responsiveness and bandage our pricked hearts with prayerless pride, we resist our Father's healing touch and kill a good hug.

How Do I Sin Against Thee? Let Me Count the Ways

A. W. Tozer has said that the church today is plagued by a low view of God.[4] I would add that our low view of God stands hand in hand with a distressingly low view of sin. Too few of us take sin seriously—particularly *our own* sin.

Our self-absorbed culture exalts assertiveness, affirmation, and self-actualization. Success in life is credited as much to a self-assured image as to skill, determination, diligence, humility, or grace. Catchy sound bites counsel us to "Believe in Yourself!" and "Never Let 'em See Ya Sweat!" Such advice does little to foster repentance of sin. Repentance does not come by believing in ourselves and projecting confidence. We are the problem—which is why the Bible commands us to confess our sins regularly and take pains to forsake them.

This principle became abundantly clear to me during the year my pastor devoted to teaching us how to pray directly from Scripture. We dedicated successive Wednesday nights to the four letters in the ACTS acrostic. Even though we prayed each week for the needs of our congregation, we concentrated each Wednesday on adoration, confession, thanksgiving, or supplication. As you may have guessed, our lowest attendance was *always* on the nights dedicated to prayers of confession. And those who did come found sincere participation to be difficult and uncomfortable.

This "confession-avoidance" may be traced to our having

accepted—consciously or unconsciously—our culture's assertion that we need high self-esteem to live as well-adjusted
people, which confession of sin does nothing to foster. But
perhaps our *real* need is to ask, "Well adjusted to what?"
Prideful self-esteem certainly does not make us well adjusted to Scripture's clear standards! Confession of sin is
what fosters a walk worthy of our high calling in Christ.

God calls His children to humble themselves (James
4:5–10; 1 Peter 5:6–11) and pursue righteousness as it is
defined in His Word (Isaiah 51:1; 1 Timothy 6:11; 2 Timothy 2:22). The only way we can do that is by seeking the
Holy Spirit's assistance in identifying our sins, repenting,
and confessing them in prayer (Psalm 19:14; 139:23–24;
James 5:5–10; 1 Peter 4:6–7).

Most of us—as fallen sinners, and as people desensitized
by our self-centered culture—go through our daily routines
oblivious to how fully sin permeates our lives. We pray,
"Lord, forgive me my sins" without getting specific and thus
deceive ourselves into thinking we have "confessed and
been forgiven" when we have not.

True confession of sin follows heart-felt repentance of
specifically identified sins. And because the problem is in
us, that can't be done without the Spirit's help. David rec-
ognized this truth when he closed his great psalm extolling
God's sovereign authority and love with the words,

> Search me, O God, and know my heart;
> Try me and know my anxious thoughts;
> And see if there be any hurtful way in me,
> And lead me in the everlasting way.
> (Psalm 139:23–24)

If you are serious about walking worthy of your high calling in Christ, do not wait another minute to pray that
prayer. But be forewarned that the result may be painful.

God's Spirit will likely astound you with the extent of your sinfulness—so that you will also be astounded by the depth of His grace. When He does show you your sin, guard your heart against unresponsiveness. Stiff kids miss out on the blessings of forgiveness and cleansing that always follow genuine confession of sin.

The Cleansing Forgiveness of Prayer

As we submit to the convicting work of the Spirit who lives in us, the truth of 1 John 1:9 becomes increasingly precious: "If we confess our sins, He is faithful and righteous to forgive us our sins and to cleanse us from all unrighteousness." With that promise the apostle John applies God's healing balm to the stinging sore of our guilt.

Confessing our sin means agreeing with God about every aspect of it. We agree, first, that we actually committed the sin, without making excuses or shifting blame to another (Psalm 51:3). We also agree that our sinful behavior offends God and violates all He intends us to be as His children (Psalm 51:4–5). We acknowledge our tendency to deny our sin, as well as God's faithfulness in driving us to repentance (Psalm 32:3–4). We admit that our sin has disrupted our fellowship with Him and that He alone can cleanse and restore us (Psalm 51:7–13). And finally we anticipate, in agreement with His revealed truth, the delightful blessings resulting from sincere confession (Psalm 32:1–2, 8–11; 51:14–19).

First John 1:9 is chock-full of comfort for even the stiffest of God's guilty kids. I often wonder when I read it if John was thinking of the way Jesus, on the night of His death, comforted a stiff kid named Peter. The disciples had gathered for their last meal together and soon found themselves under conviction for the sin of pride. None wanted to humble himself to wash the feet of the others. But all must have been horrified when Jesus quietly accepted the task they had spurned.

I'm sure you could have heard a ripe fig drop in the courtyard as the Master made His way around the room with basin and towel. The silence was broken, as it customarily was, by the burly fisherman whose stiff unresponsiveness to his Savior's tender conviction reverberated in his cry, "Never shall You wash my feet!" (John 13:8).

Jesus' great love for Peter came through in His persistent pursuit of conviction: "If I do not wash you, you have no part with Me." These words finally softened Peter. "Lord," he replied humbly, "not my feet only, but also my hands and my head" (v. 8–9).

Jesus went on to bless Peter with the comfort of His cleansing forgiveness. By assuring His repentant disciple that he did not need a bath, but only a footwashing (v. 10), He *reassured* him of his secure position among God's children. Although his stiffness had temporarily disrupted the harmony of this eternal relationship, humble confession of sin was all it took to restore it.

Notes

1. Steve Brown, *Approaching God: How to Pray* (Nashville: Moorings, 1996), 20.

2. Ibid.

3. For an in-depth discussion of our ability to overcome the allure of sin in the power of the Spirit, see the sixth chapter of Romans. There Paul assures us that even though sin remains a very real factor in our earthly lives, it's *power to control us* has been broken by our union with Christ.

4. A. W. Tozer, *The Knowledge of the Holy* (San Francisco: Harper and Row, 1961), 1.

Exercises

Review

1. Have *you* ever tried to hug a stiff kid? If so, what was it like? Describe what unresponsiveness does to our relationship with God.

2. Describe the process theologians call "imputation" and explain how it affects our relationship with God.

3. If we are to walk worthy of our high calling in Christ, why must we resist the temptation to downplay the doctrine of sin? Give some examples of areas in which you need to remain alert to this temptation.

4. What is the role of repentance in redemption and sanctification? How is prayer related to repentance in these areas? How is God glorified in our repentance?

5. Explain why we Christians have a distressingly low view of sin. How does this low view of sin influence our prayers?

6. What is the meaning of "confessing our sin"? Clarify your answer with specific examples.

7. Describe how Jesus loosened up a stiff kid named Peter. How does this situation from Scripture encourage you personally in your walk with the Lord?

Application

1. *Open-Book Prayer:* In your prayer time this week, use Psalm 139 to help you confess your sins before your sovereign Father.

2. In his book *Alone with God: The Power and Passion of Prayer* ([Wheaton, Ill.: Victor, 1995], 99), John MacArthur gives the following biblical examples of sin's permeating influence:

> Sin dominates our minds (Romans 1:21).
> Sin dominates our wills (Jeremiah 44:15–17).
> Sin dominates our emotions and affections (John 3:19).
> Sin subjects us to misery (Isaiah 48:22).
> Sin brings unbelievers under Satan's control (Ephesians 2:2).
> Sin brings unbelievers under divine wrath (Ephesians 2:3).

Read each of the Scripture references listed above and consider how sin permeates people's lives in each of these areas. If necessary, read the surrounding verses to understand the reference in its context. Then, ask the Holy Spirit to reveal *specific* sins in your life that fall into the first four categories and to help you repent of and confess these sins to God. Now ask Him to burden your heart to pray for *specific* unbelievers (by name) who fall into the final two categories.

Digging Deeper

1. Consult one or more books on church history and learn all you can about the events in Martin Luther's

life that led up to his posting of "Ninety-Five Theses" on the church door in Wittenberg. From what you have learned, explain what you think motivated him to have the *first* of his theses deal with repentance.

LESSON 9

Making Our Requests Known to God

Prayer is not asking God to do my will. It is bringing myself into conformity with His will. It is asking Him to do His will and to give me the grace to enjoy it. . . . Prayer is ever and always, first and foremost, a recognition of God's majestic glory and an act of submission to it.
—John MacArthur

Not long after we were married, I launched a valiant campaign to convince my husband to sell our cozy little home and move to a bigger place. One of my most persuasive arguments (so I thought) was my *very real need* for more closet space.

Like most new husbands, he listened patiently and responded lovingly: "Hmm, dear, that sounds pretty serious. Let's take a look at that closet."

This should clinch it! I thought smugly as I marched into the bedroom and threw open the door to my severely cramped wardrobe. Frank carefully surveyed the bulging source of my discontent. Then he placed his hand sympathetically on my shoulder and looking tenderly into my eager eyes. "Honey," he said quietly. "You don't need more closet space. You need fewer clothes."

Every woman reading this knows that those were *not* the words I longed to hear! But deep in my shocked, angry spirit, I knew they were true. Later that week, after I had calmed down, I swallowed my pride and cleaned out that closet. Soon I had six cartons of clothes packed for delivery to one of Albuquerque's Christian street-ministries and could count as a blessing my "much bigger" closet.

God had used the practical counsel of a responsible husband to convict me of several sins, all of which were deeply rooted in the fertile soil of shortsighted self-centeredness. And since then, God has often reminded me of "The Great Closet Incident" whenever I pray about "needs" I haven't filtered through Scripture.

Have You Seen Your Real Needs?

Because the Fall of the human race into sin left us helplessly shortsighted and selfish, you and I need the light of God's Word to help us identify our needs. As a young bride stuffing clothes into a minuscule closet, I failed to look beyond my "felt need" for more space. Frank, however, as head of our home, had focused on a much bigger picture. His field of vision took in our yearly income, my recent enrollment in graduate school, and our desire for a family, not to mention bills we had already accumulated. His broader view enabled him to look at my crowded closet from a much different perspective and to recognize that my *real* need was for contraction, not expansion.

How easily we forget that God who declared, and thus knows, "the end from the beginning" (Isaiah 46:10) also knows the needs of His children much better than they do. How easily we presume on His grace by filling our prayers with requests conceived in shortsightedness and brought forth in pure selfishness. And how easily we sin by resorting to anger, despair, or self-pity when He declines our requests. But how easily we *could be* rejoicing in His perfect provision if we defined our needs in terms of His perspective!

Much of the apostle Paul's joy and contentment flowed from having learned to do that. He endured labors and imprisonments; beatings, lashings, and stonings; shipwrecks, near-drownings, and incalculable dangers; sleeplessness, hunger, thirst, and exposure; as well as the ongoing stress of concern for his converts (2 Corinthians 11:3–29). Still he relied on God's truth to identify the real needs for which he should pray. Having sought and been shown the "big picture" of the gospel (Acts 22:10; Galatians 1:11), he could lift his sights beyond self and rejoice in *any* circumstance that furthered the proclamation of Christ (Philippians 1:18).

When Paul submitted himself to the counsel of God, he saw the surpassing value of counting "all things to be loss" in order to know Christ Jesus as Lord (Philippians 3:8). He willingly "endured all things for the sake of those who are chosen" (2 Timothy 2:10). He refused to consider his life "of any account as dear to [him]self" in the ministry (Acts 20:24). God had promised him grace sufficient to deal with all difficulties (2 Corinthians 12:9) and abundant resources to fulfill his high calling in Christ (2 Corinthians 9:8).

Paul knew well the God whose promises lifted his sights and comforted his soul. He reminded Timothy that God had not given him "a spirit of timidity, but of power and love and discipline" (2 Timothy 1:7). He could encourage Timothy to "join with me in suffering for the gospel according to the power of God" (v. 8) *because* "I know whom I have believed and I am convinced that He is able to guard what I have entrusted to him until that day (v. 12).

Think back for a moment to lesson 4, where we learned

that a Christian's most basic need is *knowing Christ.* There we saw that knowing Christ is the way we know God, the way we know we are saved, and the way we know the debt of love we owe to our Father. We saw too that our real needs as Christians concern our relationship with God through His Son, and that those needs are revealed in the pages of Scripture. In lesson 4 we were considering the foundational principles of open-Book prayer and could not take time to identify specific needs defined in Scripture. Now we are ready to do so.

What God Says You Need

When our Wednesday fellowship group focused on praying directly from Scripture, we never lacked for passages relevant to our needs. Since the whole of God's revelation concerns our relationship with Him, we found our needs addressed on practically every page of the Bible. Our biggest problem was deciding which to include in the allotted hour!

Most of us were surprised (and humbled) to discover how very needy we are—and to realize how much God's big-picture definition of needs differs from our typically short-sighted and selfish perceptions. What follows is a brief sampling of what God says our needs are. Read them carefully, devoting enough time to ponder the references, and see if your reaction is the same as was ours.

Aside from our most basic need of knowing Christ Jesus our Lord (Luke 10:38–42; Philippians 3:8–11), the Bible also describes our need to understand the truths contained in the Bible (2 Timothy 3:15–17), to respond to the leading of the indwelling Holy Spirit (John 15:26–27; 16:7–11; Romans 8:9–17, 26–27), and to spend time in prayer (Jeremiah 29:11–13; Luke 18:1; 1 Thessalonians 5:17).

Scripture speaks of our need for wisdom (James 1:5),

contentment (Philippians 4:11–13), and freedom from fear (Psalm 37). It tells us we need to lift our minds from the things of earth to the things above (Colossians 3:1–3), seek God's kingdom first (Matthew 6:33), and testify boldly of the gospel of grace (Ephesians 6:18–19). It highlights our need to accurately assess our abilities (Romans 12:3) and to faithfully exercise our gifts in the body of Christ (vv. 4–7).

It reveals our need to be loved by God and pass His love on to others (1 John 4:7–19), to live in relationships (Colossians 3:18–4:1; Hebrews 10:24–25), and to work for a living (2 Thessalonians 3:7–12). It exposes our need for forgiveness (Luke 18:13), as well as our need to forgive others (Ephesians 4:32), and reminds us of our need to take every thought captive to the obedience of Christ (2 Corinthians 10:5) so that no unwholesome word will proceed from our mouths (Ephesians 4:29).

Scripture also affirms our need for food, shelter, and clothing (Matthew 6:11; 1 Timothy 5:8; 6:10), and protection from danger (2 Thessalonians 3:1–2), without downplaying our concomitant need to trust in God's sovereign mercy when we must suffer deprivation or persecution for the sake of the gospel (Matthew 5:10–12; 1 Peter 2:20–24).

Were you able to see from the Scriptures God's eternal perspective in each of these needs? Did you notice that none of them derive from shortsighted and selfish worldly pursuits? Could you tell, from these few examples, that our real needs center on our relationship with God through His Son? If so, you have discovered the secret of Paul's joy and contentment.

The apostle prayed for real needs and knew that his God would *always* supply them (Philippians 4:19). He knew the indescribable peace of being anxious for nothing because his grip on God's truth gave him a big-picture perspective that transcended temporal circumstances. He would have agreed wholeheartedly with A. W. Pink, who wrote nineteen hundred years later, "There can be no peace for the mind, no joy of heart, if we fail to recognize that our lot— our circumstances, our condition—is fully ordered by a sovereign and gracious God."[1]

Praying for Others

Scripture also affirms each Christian's need to pray for others (1 Samuel 12:19, 23; Matthew 5:44; Colossians 1:9; James 5:16). Steve Brown reminds us that when we come into faith, we come into a family; and that we all seem to pray better when we pray for others than when we pray for ourselves.[2]

When you pray for others, remember that their scripturally defined needs are no different from yours, though they may experience *some* needs more intensely than you do. Praying effectively for them requires getting to know them and the particular challenges they are facing. Some people you pray for you already know intimately— your family, some relatives, close friends, and a few neighbors. But usually getting to know people takes deliberate planning, as well as a conscious investment of time and energy.

Meeting in a small group for prayer is extremely effective, particularly if you include a few people you already know and even more whom you don't. When our Wednesday group began praying together, there were several in the group I knew superficially at best. But by the end of the year, I knew them much better.

Planning get-togethers with one or two people with whom you have only a "nodding acquaintance" is also helpful. Most women these days are so busy that we tend to spend time with the same comfortable friends instead of developing relationships with those we know less well. My best friend and I agreed recently to have lunch once a month with at least one woman in our church that we don't know very well. You might prefer shopping trips, working together on gardens or crafts, or play-days in the park with other moms of young children. What you *do* is not as important as *with whom* you are doing it. These activities should be deliberately planned with the conscious intent of deepening those many relationships that haven't gotten past the surface.

You should also get to know Christians from other churches (and other denominations) in your area. You could attend or ask your leaders to host joint worship services on special occasions, or to organize community service projects together. And to help you pray for national or world-wide ministries, take the time to read their newsletters.

These are just a few suggestions for getting to know people well enough to pray effectively for them. I'm sure you will soon (as soon as you tackle Review Exercise 5!) think of many more ways to do so in your particular circumstances.

Pray as Paul Prayed

Paul prayed well for other people. If he hadn't, God would not have included so many of his prayers in the Bible. We can't go wrong in praying for others if we pattern our prayers after his divinely recorded examples. Take a few moments as you finish this lesson, and read once more through the prayers of Paul recorded in appendix C, noting specifically the kinds of requests he made for others.

Were you surprised? Do Paul's prayers for others sound like yours? What did he include that you routinely omit? What did he omit that you routinely include? Do you need to make a few (perhaps several) changes in the way you pray for others? If so, please feel free to go directly to Application Exercise 3 and work on it while his example is still fresh in your mind.

Notes

1. A. W. Pink, *Gleanings from Paul: The Prayers of the Apostle* (Chicago: Moody Press, 1967), 98.

2. Steve Brown, *Approaching God: How to Pray* (Nashville: Moorings, 1996), 148, 156.

Exercises

Review

1. Explain how the introductory quotation from John MacArthur captures the essence of this lesson concerning making our requests known to God.

2. How does God's sovereignty guarantee that He knows our needs better than we do? How does knowing this fact about God influence our prayers?

3. Read 2 Corinthians 11:23–12:10 and explain how a man whose life was filled with such difficulty could consistently exhibit an attitude of contentment and joy.

4. List five or more of your scripturally defined needs (with supporting references) and explain the biblical reason for identifying each as a need.

5. Why must you get to know people well before you can pray for them well? List some specific ways *you* (in your

particular circumstances) might get to know a few people (or groups of people) better.

Application

1. *Open-Book Prayer:* This week in your prayer time, use Psalm 37 and Ephesians 4–6 to help you identify real needs for which you can pray—both for yourself and for others.

2. List what you consider to be your primary needs at the moment. Are you able to validate each of them scripturally? For each one you are able to validate, write a brief open-Book prayer making this request known to God with thanksgiving. For each one you are unable to validate scripturally, seek God's wisdom to determine if it is, in fact, a genuine need.

3. In Paul's prayers recorded in appendix C, note the requests he presents to God in behalf of other people's needs. How do his prayers for others differ from yours? (Record *specific* examples of differences.) How are they similar? (Record *specific* similarities.) What *specific* changes do you need to make in your prayers to bring them more in line with the apostle's?

Digging Deeper

1. Describe the way(s) in which striving to maintain an *eternal perspective* (keeping God's big picture in view) changes our perception of what we need.

10

The Umbrella
of Gratitude

Among the purest gifts received from God is truth. An-
other gift, almost as precious, and without which the
first would be meaningless, is our ability to grasp truth
and appreciate it. For these priceless treasures we should
be profoundly grateful; for them our thanks should rise
to the Giver of all good gifts throughout the day and in
the night seasons.   —A. W. Tozer

It rarely rains in Albuquerque. And even when it does, it seldom rains for very long. I'm sure that's why people who live here have so much trouble laying their hands on an umbrella when we *are* surprised by a real gully-washer. We use our umbrellas so infrequently, we usually forget where we've put them!

My dear friend Lisa, however, *never* seems to lose touch with her umbrella. She lives in Seattle. Need I say more? The climate in which she lives keeps that umbrella ever close at hand and never far from her thoughts.

Umbrellas are protective devices. Their primary purpose is shielding us from an array of distressing environmental bombardments. And the *umbrella of gratitude* serves that very same purpose in prayer.

Why Our Prayers Need Protecting

Prayer may well be the most fragile of all God-given means of grace. I say that not because prayer itself is weak, but because its effectiveness depends largely on the attitudes and wills of very weak people. Even though our transformation in Christ broke the controlling power of sin (Romans 6:17–19) and turned our hearts toward obeying God, it did not *eliminate* our ability—or our desire—to succumb to temptation (1 Corinthians 10:12; Hebrews 12:4; James 4:7).

We have seen in previous lessons that God has fully equipped us to resist the allure of the world, the flesh, and the Devil. And God requires us to make deliberate use of that equipment in full view of His enemies. When done well, prayer is a most powerful tool in God's service. For that very reason, it is a prime target of Satan.

As temporary Prince of This World, he attacks prayer quite successfully by raining down discouragement and distraction on God's children. The *time* believers need to pray can be eroded by a flood of "essential" activities. And the still, small voice of the Spirit calling Christians to commune with their Father can easily be drowned out by the rushing cacophony of busy schedules. And the hope that should draw us often to God's throne in prayer can be immersed in anxieties produced by life's pressures.

If our prayers are to function as God intended, they must be shielded from environmental bombardment that dilutes devotion and washes away hope. The umbrella of gratitude serves that purpose well.

The Shielding Quality of Gratitude

In lesson 4, I rearranged the letters in the familiar ACTS acrostic to spell TACS, written like this:

$$A\!\!\!\;T\;{C \atop S}$$

My motive for rearranging that time-honored acrostic was that in all the years I had used it, I never could isolate "thanksgiving" in my prayers. As I began devoting more time to praying with others, I noticed they couldn't either. No matter how hard we tried to fence in our thanksgiving, it kept stretching over the other divisions of prayer.

Apparently, I wasn't the only one having a hard time confessing my sin and receiving forgiveness without also expressing gratitude for those privileges of grace. Certainly I was not alone in my impulse to thank God every time I voiced my requests to Him. In fact, almost every Christian with whom I'd prayed found it nearly impossible to adore God in prayer without slipping in a few dozen "thank you's."

These observations awakened several inquisitive brain cells, which led me to wonder, *Perhaps thanksgiving isn't a distinct category of prayer, after all. Perhaps it would be better depicted as the* environment *in which adoration, confession, and supplication take place.*

But soon a hoard of more analytical brain cells fired up and rerouted my thinking. *No, that's not it! The actual environment of prayer is the worldly realm in which Christians walk as living sacrifices, tenaciously testifying of God's goodness and grace. Thanksgiving is more a mindset or attitude that* shields *prayer from the onslaught of distraction and discouragement within that environment.*

My precious few wise brain cells stroked their gray beards and confirmed my suspicions. *Thanksgiving is more than one of prayer's categories!*

As I approach two decades of union with Christ, I have never been more aware of the persistent joint efforts of the world, the flesh, and the Devil to keep me from praying. But I am rejoicing (brain cells one and all) in this new perspective on gratitude. The umbrella of gratitude provides me—and you—with a great deal of protection against a hostile environment.

How Gratitude Protects Prayer

The Oxford Dictionary defines gratitude as "being thankful; readiness to show appreciation for and to return kindness."[1] This definition is fully consistent with the Bible's use of the term.[2] It also reveals why thanksgiving is perfectly suited to shielding our prayers against environmental bombardment.

Read the definition again and note that the essence of gratitude is *active appreciation* for kindness received. Genuine gratitude does more than sit still and emote. It isn't satisfied with warm, fuzzy feelings. It is compelled to take action. Genuine gratitude works at *demonstrating* its appreciation by returning the favor.

We would be hard put to find a better description of the *transforming* nature of our redemption. God saves us by His grace, and in return for His kindness our transformed hearts offer grateful obedience. As one wise soul put it concisely, "Theology is grace. . . . Ethics is gratitude."

Satan knows that he cannot undo the redemptive work of God. And so he seeks to undermine God's purposes by sidelining His saints. Since our service is fueled by the fires of thanksgiving, Satan presses *his* agenda by sowing seeds of ingratitude.

Do you recall how he instigated the Fall of humanity? He insinuated to Eve in the Garden that God's "kindness" to them had stopped short of full blessing. God was, after all, withholding knowledge that would make them like Him. By focusing Eve's eyes on the one thing God *hadn't* given her, Satan was able to distract her attention from all He *had* given her. Seeds of ingratitude, once sown, quickly take root and sprout. The woman immediately disobeyed God, persuaded her husband to join her, and plunged the whole human race into total depravity (see Genesis 3:1–6).

I'm sure you are no stranger to this tactic. Neither am I. How many times throughout the day are we tempted to shift our sights from our blessings to the things we don't have? How many times have we watered seeds of ingratitude from a cesspool of discontent? How many failures in service could we trace directly to a lack of thanksgiving? And how many of our "prayers" have fallen flat for lack of grateful hearts?

Knowing that Satan takes aim at our prayers, we can defend against his attack by covering those prayers with thanksgiving. The umbrella of gratitude concentrates our attention on the goodness of God. It fills our minds with His glory (adoration), humbles our souls with His grace (confession), and inspires our hope with His promises (supplication). The umbrella of gratitude turns our eyes away from the world and uproots discontentment. Gratitude *itself* (thanksgiving) fosters deeper gratitude, building an impermeable shield around the hearts of the saints.

We should not be surprised then, that Satan hates grateful prayer. He hates it so much, in fact, that he'll stop at nothing to kill it. He'll flood us with worry, stress us out with activity, or entertain us to death. He'll whisper that we have it too rough to give thanks. He'll suggest that our real satisfaction flows from this world, not from the gracious hand of our Father. Or he'll convince us that grace is cheap and not worthy of our gratitude. He'll do anything in his power to drain our hearts of grateful dependence on God so that there is no point in devotion to prayer.

So, what are we to do? How can we very weak people protect our fragile prayers against Satan's onslaught? Let me see now, where did I put that umbrella . . . ?

Building an Umbrella of Gratitude

We have seen that thanksgiving protects prayer, and that thankful prayer generates deeper thanksgiving. But how do we get started? How do we build an umbrella of gratitude? Are there other spiritual disciplines that can help us develop an attitude of thanksgiving?

The book of Acts defines the life of the church in terms of four essential spiritual disciplines. The early Christians devoted themselves to the apostles' teaching, fellowship, Communion, and prayer (Acts 2:42). Pursuing each of these disciplines produces thanksgiving and thus helps us build our umbrella of gratitude.

The *teaching* contained in the Bible provides the umbrella's skeletal framework. As we grow in our knowledge of God's truth, our umbrella takes shape and gains strength, providing a solid basis for our grateful response to our Father's care.

Fellowship is the fabric that—firmly attached to the framework of scriptural knowledge—gives our umbrella its practical usefulness. When God's Word is lived out in His covenant community, the bond of mutual encouragement and corporate thanksgiving helps God's people withstand the world, the flesh, and the Devil.

Celebrating *Communion* stimulates thanksgiving by giving us a tangible reminder of God's covenant promises. It may be seen as our umbrella's handle. Connecting us both to God and to each another, it gives us something to hold on to in the midst of life's storms.

When we devote ourselves to these spiritual disciplines, *prayer* becomes more natural, generating even more gratitude, and giving us greater strength against the Evil One. *All* of the vital functions of the body of Christ work together to promote adoration, confession, and supplication under the umbrella of gratitude.

Paul's Umbrella of Gratitude

In at least one respect, the apostle Paul reminds me of my dear friend Lisa: he never forgot where he put his umbrella.

Paul's prayers were well shielded against his stormy environment. If you look again at his prayers in appendix C, you will find them remarkably unscathed by the assaults he endured. Though Paul served God in decidedly hostile surroundings, his prayers don't reflect distress about that. Instead, they pulsate with the steady heartbeat of thanksgiving.

Paul expresses thanks for the world-renowned testimony of the Romans' faith and for their freedom from sin (Romans 1:8; 6:17–18). He thanks God for the grace and enrichment He bestowed on the believers in Corinth (1 Corinthians 1:4–9); and for the sweet aroma of Christ in every place, the earnestness of Titus, and God's indescribable gift (2 Corinthians 2:14; 8:16; 9:15).

He never ceases giving thanks for God's work at Ephesus (Ephesians 1:15–19), Philippi (Philippians 1:3–5), and Colosse (Colossians 1:3–6); and reminds the Thessalonians in his first letter of his gratitude for their work of faith, labor of love, and steadfastness of hope in response to God's Word (1 Thessalonians 1:2–4; 2:3). In his second letter to them, he reiterates his thankfulness for the way they lived out their faith in the Lord (2 Thessalonians 1:3; 2:13). And in other letters, we find similar expressions of gratitude for God's work in the lives of his friends Timothy and Philemon (2 Timothy 1:3; Philemon 4–6).

Paul's environment made him acutely aware of his dependence on the umbrella of gratitude. No wonder he kept it within easy reach! But Paul reminds us that our situation is not all that different from his. Under persistent attack from the world, the flesh, and the Devil, we must "be anxious for nothing, but in everything by prayer and supplication *with thanksgiving* let our requests be made known to God." Then we will know incomprehensible peace (Philippians 4:6–7).

As the pressure around us intensifies, it should remind us of our constant need for knowledge of the truth (2 Timothy 2:15; 3:16–17), fellowship (Hebrews 10:24–25), Communion (1 Corinthians 11:26), and unceasing prayer (1 Thessalonians 5:17). If we remember these, we will be less likely to forget where we stashed our umbrellas. And with that protection always close at hand, we will be more likely to heed Paul's admonition: "Devote yourselves to prayer, keeping alert in it with an attitude of thanksgiving" (Colossians 4:2).

Notes

1. *The Oxford Dictionary and Thesaurus: American Edition* (New York, Oxford: Oxford University Press, 1996), 641.

2. The Hebrew word *yadah* and its derivative *todah* carry the idea of public declaration or acknowledgment. The Greek words *eucharisteō, eucharistos,* and *eucharistia* signify a thankful attitude and a demonstration of gratitude.

Exercises

Review

1. Describe our need for an umbrella of gratitude. What other purposes might such an umbrella serve, aside from protecting prayer?

2. Explain my motivation for rearranging the ACTS acrostic. How do the two acrostics portray differently the role of thanksgiving in prayer? Which acrostic comes closer to representing your experience in prayer?

3. Define *gratitude*. Based on your definition, explain how gratitude is well suited to shield prayer from environmental bombardment.

4. How does Satan use ingratitude to accomplish his purposes?

5. Explain how all four spiritual disciplines described in Acts 2:42 work together to build our umbrellas of gratitude.

6. How might following Paul's example (1 Corinthians 11:1; Philippians 3:17) help us heed his admonition concerning prayer in Colossians 4:2?

Application

1. *Open-Book Prayer:* In your prayer time this week, use Psalm 19:7–14, Galatians 5:25–6:10, Luke 22:1–20, and Colossians 4:2 to help you construct a strong umbrella of gratitude.

2. List several specific environmental assaults that routinely distract you from effective prayer. Then describe how (1) gaining a more thorough knowledge of Scripture, (2) being stimulated to love and good works by fellowship with believers, and (3) participating appropriately (see 1 Corinthians 11:17–31) in Communion would shield your prayers from these particular assaults. How would prayer enhance the protection provided by these

other means? (Be sure to identify *specific* deterrents to *your* prayers.)

3. Read 2 Corinthians 11:23–12:10 and explain how these verses reveal Paul's effective use of his umbrella of gratitude. Then explain how following his example will help you become more proficient in using yours.

Digging Deeper

1. Relate the words of A. W. Tozer that introduced this lesson to what you have learned about the umbrella of gratitude.

11

Great Expectations

When the Bible speaks of praying in faith, it does not mean having faith in prayer. . . .Our faith is not to be in the hope that we can pray well enough, nor in the assumption that the theoretical "laws" of prayer will work if we do. —John Blanchard

What would you say to a friend who has just told you she's lost faith in prayer?

If you had read carefully and understood the wise words of John Blanchard, your first response would be, "Good!" Then, having caught her attention, you could explain that great expectations in prayer do not spring from having faith in our prayers, but from having faith in our Father and in His revealed Word.

If your friend is a Christian, she would probably agree and quickly backtrack on her choice of words. What she *really* meant was that she was disappointed, discouraged, and frustrated because her prayers seem so futile. After all, she has prayed often and earnestly that God would grant her the desires of her heart. But nothing has happened, and she is ready to quit.

Now what would you say?

May I suggest that you take her to Scripture? She may need a reminder of what God says to His children about great expectations in prayer.

How to Get What You Pray For

Disappointment, discouragement, and frustration in prayer almost always occur when we don't see results. We pray our hearts out expecting "great things from a great God," and we can't understand why that great God does nothing. We try a variety of new methods. We pray longer and harder. But nothing we do seems to "move" God to action. Before long we conclude that prayer is not worth the effort.

If only someone could tell us how to get what we pray for. Well, I have good news. Somebody has. Listen to what John, the beloved apostle of Jesus, says to us in his first letter: "And this is the confidence which we have before Him, that, if we ask anything according to His will, He hears us. And if we know that He hears us in whatever we ask, we know that we have the requests which we have asked from Him" (1 John 5:14–15).

I doubt if anyone could have expressed it more clearly. If we ask *anything* in keeping with God's will, we can *know* for a fact that we'll get what we pray for. "Yes, but . . ." I hear someone saying. "There's a huge catch in that verse. Before I can pray with great expectations, I must discover God's will!"

Yes, that is true. But it's not a "huge catch." Finding God's will is *not* terribly difficult. Our loving Father hasn't hidden it from us.

I Found It!

Many Christians approach "finding God's will" as if they were playing the childhood game Hide and Seek. They assume that God hides His will and then requires us to seek it. But try as I may, I can't find any support in Scripture for that idea. God's will for His children is not hidden. It is clearly revealed in the pages of Scripture. We don't need to hunt for it. We need only to read and understand it.

We can locate the passages where God's will is discussed by consulting an exhaustive concordance and by checking the cross-references of the verses we find. One thing we'll soon notice is that God's will falls into two distinct categories.

The first is God's *secret will,* His sovereign plan for all that happens, which He has decreed from before the creation of the world. The Westminster Shorter Catechism describes God's decrees as "His eternal purpose, according to the counsel of *His will,* whereby, for His own glory, He hath foreordained whatsoever comes to pass" (Q/A 7, my emphasis). A striking reference to this appears in Ephesians 1:11. There Paul describes our inheritance in Christ as "having been predestined according to His purpose who works all things after the counsel of *His will.*"

This secret will is indeed largely hidden from our view. But there is a second kind of will of God, one that we have in plain view: God's *revealed will,* His commands. Deuteronomy 29:29 says, "The secret things belong to the LORD our God, but the things revealed belong to us and to our sons forever, that we may observe all the words of this law." In other words, God has spelled out how He wants us to live. And what God has not told us, we don't need to know.

It is in God's revealed will, made plain in the commands of Scripture, that we learn how to live and what we should desire. Examples of God's revealed requirements can be found in Exodus 20:1–17, Matthew 22:37–40, Romans

12:1–2, Ephesians 4:17–5:7, 1 Thessalonians 4:3–6, 1 Peter 2:13–15, and the entire book of James. While our prayers should express faith in God's hidden, sovereign plan for all things, God directs us to pray particularly for what we know to be His revealed will. That will is not hidden from us. It stands in full view throughout the pages of Scripture.

As you study Scripture, you'll notice that God's revealed will appears as broad general principles, not specific directives for every circumstance. You will not find a verse saying, "Marry Bob instead of Bill, Harry, or Sam." Nor will you find one specifying that you should move to Seattle, enroll at Ole Miss, or retire in six months. What you will find are the necessary *guidelines* within which you can make such decisions with Spirit-led wisdom. Remember, the Holy Spirit always works through the Word (see lesson 7).

God's Guidelines for Prayer

The only way to pray with great expectations is to pray within the guidelines of God's revealed will. I have identified the following six:

The first we could call the *guideline of salvation*. Only those who have been redeemed and transformed by the power of God have the ability to discover God's will for their lives. First Corinthians 2:6–16 affirms that the "mind of Christ" is essential for understanding "all that God has prepared for those who love Him" (v. 9). The unredeemed can know only that God desires their salvation (1 Timothy 2:3–4; 2 Peter 3:9) and commands their repentance (Acts 2:38; 3:19; 26:20). A fuller knowledge of His will for their lives can come only after the Spirit has brought them to salvation.

The *guideline of dependence* reminds us of our need to rely continually on the indwelling Spirit (Ephesians 5:17).

Although we have been made complete in Christ (Colossians 2:10), we remain able to grieve the Spirit by quenching His leading (Ephesians 4:30; 1 Thessalonians 5:19). And when we do that, we are left highly vulnerable to being taken "captive through philosophy and empty deception, according to the tradition of men, [and] . . . the elementary principles of the world" (Colossians 2:8). Praying with wisdom and discernment requires that we live in conscious dependence on and communion with the Spirit of Christ.

The *guideline of holiness* is crucial because it is so comprehensive. Found in 1 Thessalonians 4:3, it states, "This is the will of God, your sanctification." Sanctification is the process by which we are set apart for God's service and grow in Christlikeness. It begins when we're saved and continues until we are glorified in heaven. It therefore includes every step of our walk with the Lord.

Each decision we make should be considered in the light of this guideline. We need to ask prayerfully, "Which action will best further God's kingdom? Which will help me grow to be more like my Savior?" Often those questions point to one clear pathway. But occasionally they reveal that we're free to choose from among several good alternatives.

The *guideline of testimony* can be found in 1 Peter 2:9–17. Peter tells us that we are "a chosen race, a royal priesthood, a holy nation, a people for God's own possession, that [we] may proclaim the excellencies of Him who has called [us] out of darkness into His marvelous light" (v. 9). God has saved us and left us in the world as "aliens and strangers" (v. 11) so that our behavior can be observed and bring Him glory (v. 12). "For such is the will of God," Peter says, "that by doing right you may silence the ignorance of foolish men" (v. 15). As we pray over decisions, we should ask God to help us determine which course of action will glorify Him the most.

The *guideline of sacrifice* is the most difficult. We all prefer to walk the path of least suffering. But Romans 12:1–2 commands us to present ourselves to God as living and holy sacrifices. We do that by shunning conformity to the world and "be[ing] transformed by the renewing of [our] minds," which proves that the will of God is good, acceptable, and perfect.

Nothing confirms God's transforming work like a believer's righteous response to hardship. That is why James tells us to "consider it all joy" when we encounter trials (1:2);[1] and why Peter tell us to "entrust [our] souls to a faithful Creator in doing what is right" when we "suffer according to the will of God" (1 Peter 4:19). This guideline urges us to pray for the willingness and ability to walk as worthily on the hard paths as we do on the easy ones.

Finally, the *guideline of sovereignty* encompasses the other five guidelines. It reminds us that God alone knows the end from the beginning and that He will accomplish all His good pleasure (Isaiah 46:10). In doing so, it reaffirms that the purpose of prayer is not to "move" God to act as we would desire, but to discern His good will for our lives and to submit ourselves to it.

What Should We Expect?

When we pray within these scriptural guidelines, we will be able to "claim the promise" the apostle John made to us. Disappointment, discouragement, and frustration will have no room to fester when our prayers swell with the confidence of great expectations. If we align our prayers with God's will, we will see results.

The most striking result is that *God will be glorified.* Jesus tells us in John 14:13 that when we ask in His name (that is, according to His will—see lesson 6), He will do it, "that the Father may be glorified in the Son." Answered prayer thus becomes a dramatic display His many glorious attributes. Our prayers should be expectant enough to offer God the largest possible stage on which to enact His glory.

Another result is that *the elect will be brought to salvation.* Paul's example compels us to pray for the salvation of sinners (Romans 9:3; 10:1). Even though neither our prayers nor our actions are sufficient to "save" anyone, God has chosen to use both mysteriously as key means of bringing His chosen children into His family. Our prayers sweeten the fragrance that draws elect unbelievers to Christ (2 Corinthians 2:14).

A third result is that *we will see a developing pattern of righteousness* in our own lives and the lives of others for whom we pray. As we confess our sins and receive God's cleansing forgiveness in prayer, we will see evidence of the practical outworking of our transformation in Christ (2 Corinthians 3:18).

Fourth, as we "bear one another's burdens" (Galatians 6:1–5) and encourage each other (Hebrews 10:24–25) in prayer, *the body of Christ will be built up and will bear fruit* abundantly. Jesus said, "I chose you, and appointed you, that you should go and bear fruit, and that your fruit should remain" (John 15:16). Fruitfulness is a direct result of praying—and living—according to God's will. First John 3:21–22 describes the way obedience underscores confident prayer: "Beloved, if our heart does not condemn us, we have confidence before God; and whatever we ask we receive from Him, because we keep His commandments and do the things that are pleasing in His sight."

Two more results are that *our hearts will be full of peace, joy and contentment;* and *we will know God's comfort in the midst of affliction.* When our prayers long for God's will, we find it much easier to be content in all circumstances (Philippians 4:11–13). We can rest assured knowing that His purposes work out for both His glory and our benefit (Psalm 37).

Jesus said in John 16:24 that if we ask in His name, our joy will be "made full." Paul assures us in Philippians 4:6–7 that when we make our requests known to our Father, "the peace of God, which surpasses all comprehension, shall guard [our] hearts and minds in Christ Jesus." Even when God's will for our lives includes difficulty and heartache, Paul assures us that we'll receive more than enough comfort to share with others who suffer (2 Corinthians 1:3–7).

Perhaps the greatest result of praying for God's will is this: *we will become increasingly able to "set [our] mind on the things above, not on the things that are on earth"* (Colossians 3:2). Nothing gives us a more heavenly focus than seeking in earnest prayer to know and live in God's will.

Notes

1. See my study *James on Trials: How Faith Matures in the Storms of Life* (Los Alamos, N.M.: Deo Volente Publishing, 1998), for an in-depth discussion of how Christians should face trials.

Exercises

Review

1. Have you ever experienced disappointment, discouragement, or frustration in prayer? Describe the situation that produced these feelings and determine whether they were indeed caused by a "lack of results."

2. How can we be sure that we'll get what we pray for?

3. Distinguish between God's secret will and His revealed will. Can you think of at least one example of each?

4. How does God reveal His will to us? Describe six specific examples.

5. Describe several "great expectations" of prayer that are produced by aligning our wills with God's will.

6. Suppose a friend has recently written you a letter in which she told you she has lost faith in prayer. Respond to her letter explaining why you are glad she has done so.

Application

1. *Open-Book Prayer:* This week in your prayer time use Psalm 37; Ephesians 4:1–6:20; and/or 1 Peter 2:9–17; 4:1–19 to help you discern God's will for specific decisions.

2. Describe a current situation in your life in which you are attempting to discern God's will regarding a decision you face. If you have not yet done so, consult the Scriptures to see if God's will for your situation is specifically stated. (An obvious example would be if you were trying to discern God's will regarding whether you should engage in an extramarital affair!) If you are new to studying the Bible, get some help from an exhaustive concordance or wise leaders and friends. If you do not find *direct guidance* for your decision, look for Scriptures that will help you answer the following questions:

   – Do I have the mind of Christ, which I need to understand God's truth? In other words, upon what am I basing my assurance of salvation? (This assurance should be grounded in Scripture rather than feelings.)
   – How will the Holy Spirit assist me in making this decision? What must I do to gain the most benefit from His assistance?

- Which alternative(s) will further God's kingdom on earth? If more than one alternative will do so, will one or two further God's kingdom *more* than the others?
- Which alternatives will help me become more like Jesus Christ?
- Which alternatives will best put God's attributes on display in the world?
- Which alternatives are appealing simply because they minimize suffering? Which ones will enhance my ability to walk as worthily on hard paths as on easy ones?
- Which alternatives lift my eyes from the earth to heaven?
- What *should* I do in this situation?
- What *will* I do in this situation?
- How will I carry out my decision?

3. If you are not currently seeking to discern God's will for a particular decision, use those questions to rethink a decision you made in the past. Based upon your evaluation, do you believe you made the best decision? Explain, supporting your answer with Scripture.

Digging Deeper

1. Some people have reasoned that God's sovereignty must be limited to His secret will, expressed in decrees (His "decretive will"), since His revealed commands (His "preceptive will") require human obedience. Refute this line of reasoning from Scripture, citing specific examples of how God's sovereignty is expressed through both aspects of His will.

12

A Divine Blueprint for Prayer

The potency of prayer has subdued the strength of fire, it has bridled the rage of lions, hushed anarchy to rest, extinguished wars, appeased the elements, expelled demons, burst the chains of death, expanded the gates of heaven, assuaged diseases, dispelled frauds, rescued cities from destruction, stayed the sun in its course, and arrested the progress of the thunderbolt. There is an all-sufficient panoply, a treasure undiminished, a mine which is never exhausted, a sky unobscured by clouds, a heaven unruffled by the storm. It is the root, the fountain, the mother of a thousand blessings.

—John Chrysostom

You may have found it odd that so far I've scarcely mentioned the pattern for prayer Jesus taught His disciples in Matthew 6:9–13. Well, I've done that on purpose, and it hasn't been easy! But I've worked hard to do so for what I believe is a very good reason.

The pattern for prayer Jesus taught His disciples is, without doubt, *the* perfect illustration of almost everything we have learned so far in this study. Unfortunately, most of us are so thoroughly familiar with its masterful phrasing that we easily miss its illustrative impact. And that is why I have intentionally kept it under wraps until this lesson. As we unveil it now in review of what we have learned, may God's Holy Spirit impress us afresh with its glorious depth.

Take a Good Look

Perhaps the best way to begin is to step back and take a wide-angle view of this marvelous passage. Try to read these beloved words of your Savior as if you've never read them before. Deliberately slow your mind so that you can ponder them carefully:

> Our Father who art in heaven,
> Hallowed be Thy name.
> Thy kingdom come.
> Thy will be done,
> On earth as it is in heaven.
> Give us this day our daily bread.
> And forgive us our debts, as we also have
>   forgiven our debtors.
> And do not lead us into temptation, but deliver
>   us from evil.
> [For Thine is the kingdom, and the power, and
>   the glory, forever.
> Amen.]

Now open your Bible and read these verses again in the context of Jesus' Sermon on the Mount. If you have time, read the entire sermon (Matthew 5:1–7:29), but if you do not, read at least Matthew 5:43–6:18.

If you have read carefully, you may have detected two

significant points. First, the most common title of this passage—"The Lord's Prayer"—is a bit of a misnomer. Because our Lord is sinless, He would never have prayed "in this way"; and technically, the passage is more a *guideline* for prayer than a prayer in itself. What we have here is a divine blueprint drawn by the Lord to help His disciples pray as God intended.[1]

Second, you have probably noticed that the context has to do with the *purpose* of prayer. Jesus leaves no doubt in His sermon that prayer is a part of the *practice of righteousness* by which we "are to be perfect, as [our] heavenly Father is perfect" (Matthew 5:48–6:1). As such, prayer must focus on Him, not ourselves.

A key theme of the Sermon on the Mount concerns how our righteousness glorifies God in the world (5:16, 20, 48; 6:24, 33; 7:12, 21, 24–27). Jesus warns His disciples of "practicing [their] righteousness before men" (6:1). "Righteousness" done for show exalts men, not God. To make sure His disciples get the point, Jesus gives them three examples of how righteous acts (alms giving, prayer, and fasting) can easily degenerate into self-exaltation. It is in His second example that He presents them with the perfect pattern for prayer. When used with understanding, that blueprint prevents us from praying self-centeredly.

Jesus' prayer pattern is perfect because it draws our attention to the will of the Father. It calls us to lift our eyes to heaven and to look at our world through the lens of God's revealed purposes. Only then can we ask with right motives and know we'll receive the very best of God's gifts according to His riches in glory (James 4:1–3; 1 Corinthians 1:4–9; Ephesians 3:16; Philippians 4:19).

The previous eleven lessons in our study have emphasized the importance of a Godward focus in prayer. Knowing that our fallen natures lean toward self-centeredness, we desperately need to be reminded of that. Having a Godward focus in prayer will never be easy as long as we live in the depraved state known as "the flesh." But focusing on God becomes an increasingly normal response as we are filled with God's Spirit (Romans 8:5–8).

Family Privilege Revisited

Jesus' pattern for prayer begins with the two words, "Our Father"—a love-laced allusion to the privilege of family. As God's chosen children, secure in His love, we may approach His throne boldly (though not arrogantly) and make our requests known to Him with confidence.

The phrase, "who art in heaven," assures us of His divine power and wisdom. He isn't just any father; He is *God, our* Father, who is both sovereign and gracious. Thus, our bold, confident prayers are inspired by the knowledge that His loving desire to care for His children will be accomplished (Isaiah 46:10). We pray with the assurance that He alone has the ability, as well as the desire, to meet our every need perfectly.

Psalm 37 exalts God's perfect provision as it reminds us to rejoice in our great privilege of family:

> Trust in the LORD, and do good;
> Dwell in the land and cultivate faithfulness.
> Delight yourself in the LORD;
> And He will give you the desires of your heart.
> Commit your way to the LORD,
> Trust also in Him, and He will do it. . . .
> The steps of a man are established by the LORD;
> And He delights in his way.
> When he falls, he shall not be hurled headlong;
> Because the LORD is the One who holds his hand.
> I have been young, and now I am old;
> Yet I have not seen the righteous forsaken,

Or his descendants begging bread. . . .
The righteous will inherit the land,
And dwell in it forever.
The mouth of the righteous utters wisdom,
And his tongue speaks justice.
The law of his God is in his heart;
His steps do not slip. . . .
Wait for the LORD, and keep His way,
And He will exalt you to inherit the land; . . .
But the salvation of the righteous is from
    the LORD;
He is their strength in time of trouble.
And the LORD helps them, and delivers them;
He delivers them from the wicked, and
    saves them,
Because they take refuge in Him. (vv. 3–5, 23–25,
    29–31, 34, 39–40)

The blessing of prayer is an exclusive privilege of family. Our divine blueprint for prayer begins by reminding all of God's children of this most marvelous benefit.

A Refresher Course on Perspective

Jesus' pattern for prayer continues by outlining a perfectly prioritized list of requests. These requests encapsule both the righteous desires and genuine needs of God's children, whose chief business is to seek His kingdom (Matthew 6:33). The three primary requests have to do with God and His glory, and the three subordinate ones equip us for service.

This order is significant. Requests that God honors flow from a God-centered perspective. God created and saved us to give Him glory and honor, and He designed us to enjoy life most intensely when we fulfill that purpose. Thus, the requests given highest priority are those concerning God's exaltation. Since our greatest need is knowing the Lord and our greatest weakness is preoccupation with self, the first order of business in prayer is getting our eyes off ourselves and focused on Him. Our divine blueprint helps us do that by topping the list with requests asking for God's name to be hallowed, His kingdom to come, and His will to be done on earth as it is in heaven.

The word "hallow" means to sanctify (set apart), revere, or to make and keep holy. And the "name" of God encompasses everything true of Him. Therefore, requests that ask for God's name to be hallowed direct our attention to His revelation of Himself in His Word. The very best prayers for God's name to be hallowed come right out of Scripture.

Requests that ask for His kingdom to come and His will to be done on earth as in heaven demand committing our lives to His purposes. Our divine blueprint contains no provision for bringing our personal agendas to God and seeking His blessing upon them. Rather, it requires us to place ourselves at our Father's disposal for whatever service He sees fit in His kingdom.

Such prayer may seem risky, but it isn't at all. Serving God without reservation produces life's greatest blessings. We can trust Him implicitly when He tells us that He works all things together for good for those who love Him and are called according to His purpose (Romans 8:28). And we can submit without fear when we believe and rely on the promise He spoke through the prophet Jeremiah:

> "For I know the plans that I have for you," declares the LORD, "plans for welfare and not for calamity to give you a future and a hope. Then you will call upon Me and come and pray to Me, and I will listen to you. And you will seek Me and find Me, when you search for Me with all your heart." (29:11–13)

Prayer that is focused on God-centered priorities sharpens our perception of our real needs. We have seen throughout this study that our central needs concern our relationship with God through Jesus Christ. That top priority is confirmed by our divine blueprint for prayer.

One More Look at Our Needs

Jesus' pattern for prayer defines our real needs as the things we must have to fulfill God's purpose for us. If the first requests remind us that we glorify and enjoy God by hallowing His name, seeking His kingdom, and doing His will, the latter requests address what we need to accomplish those things on earth: physical sustenance, forgiveness, and guidance.

As physical beings, we need food, clothing, and shelter in order to serve God in this world. Jesus instructs us to voice these needs to our Father and not to worry about " 'What shall we eat?' or 'What shall we drink?' or 'With what shall we clothe ourselves?' " Our "heavenly Father knows that [we] need all these things" (Matthew 6:31–33). He will supply an abundance of what we need to complete the work He has given us (2 Corinthians 9:8).

In order to glorify God and enjoy Him in service, we also need His cleansing forgiveness. Stiff kids don't reflect well on their Father's goodness or exhibit the delight of being part of His family.

Our need for guidance is summed up in the request, "And do not lead us into temptation, but deliver us from evil." Although some infer from this that God tempts us to sin, our Lord's brother James flatly states otherwise: "Let no one say when he is tempted, 'I am being tempted by God'; for God cannot be tempted by evil, and He Himself does not tempt anyone. But each one is tempted when he is carried away and enticed by his own lust" (1:13–15). We can't blame temptation on God. The fault is our own.

James also knew that drawing closer to God will deliver us from all kinds of evil.

> Submit therefore to God. Resist the devil and he will flee from you. Draw near to God and He will draw near to you. Cleanse your hands, you sinners; and purify your hearts, you double-minded. Be miserable and mourn and weep; let your laughter be turned into mourning, and your joy to gloom. Humble yourselves in the presence of the Lord, and He will exalt you. (4:7–10)

Even without this corroboration from James, we can be sure that the Lord Jesus Christ would not have maligned God's immaculate character as some seem to think. This final request must be read as a plea for God's help in resisting the constant barrage of temptation assailing us from the world, our own flesh, and the Devil. We can count on His guidance through this maze of deceit because He is a compassionate Father who knows our frail frame (Psalm 103:13–14). He will not allow us to be tempted beyond what we're able (1 Corinthians 10:13).

A Final Review

The closing phrase of our divine blueprint for prayer, "For Thine is the kingdom, and the power, and the glory, forever. Amen,"[2] makes sure that we close out our prayers with our focus unblurred. Have we lost sight of God's glory in the midst of our needs? Have the things of the world dulled our commitment to the kingdom of God? Have the forces of evil clouded our view of God's power? This final vision check calls us back to that essential God-centered perspective so that we don't lose sight of our Lord's purpose for our lives and our prayers.

Notes

1. The only passage of Scripture that I think should be called "The Lord's Prayer" is John 17.

2. There is some evidence that this sentence was not in the original prayer given by our Lord, but was added later during the copying process. However, for our purposes in this study, the issue isn't critical. The sentence is an echo of 1 Chronicles 29:11, an Old Testament prayer that Jesus would certainly have known and used: "Thine, O LORD, is the greatness and the power and the glory and the victory and the majesty, indeed everything that is in the heavens and the earth; Thine is the dominion, O LORD, and Thou dost exalt Thyself as head over all."

Exercises

Review

1. Describe the context in which Jesus' pattern for prayer is found in the Bible. What, if any, new insights did you gain regarding this passage of Scripture by placing it in its context?

2. What is the significance of the opening phrase of Jesus' pattern for prayer?

3. How does Psalm 37 illustrate the great family privilege(s) of the children of God?

4. Explain how the order of the requests found in Jesus' pattern for prayer defines the proper perspective of prayer.

5. What is the primary concern of the first three requests? What is the primary concern of the next three requests? Describe how these two sets of requests relate to each other.

6. If someone were to tell you that God tempts people to sin and supported her assertion with Matthew 6:13, how would you respond?

Application

1. *Open-Book Prayer:* In your prayer time this week, use Jesus' pattern for prayer found in Matthew 6:9–13 to help you apply everything you have learned in this study to your personal prayers.

2. Describe a time in your life when you found it very difficult or even impossible to pray. What elements of the situation made praying so difficult? Write out a "prayer approach" to this situation structured according to your divine blueprint for prayer found in Matthew 6:9–13. How will such an approach help you pray in the midst of similarly difficult situations in the future? Explain your answer.

Digging Deeper

1. Consider the striking contrast between the God-centered assessment of needs contained in Jesus' pattern for prayer and the world's view of needs. Whereas Jesus says we need physical sustenance, forgiveness, and guidance, the world tells us we need security, significance, and self-esteem. Research the subject of "human needs" and explain the vast difference between these two perspectives.

13

The Pervasive Power of Prayer

The Christian's trade is prayer.   —Martin Luther

Our church in Albuquerque has come in for its fair share of criticism over the years, some of it spawning healthy changes. One recurring criticism, however, concerns a practice that our leaders appear to have no intention of changing. We're told that our worship service contains *far too much prayer.*

That never fails to astound me. But during recent months, as I've been immersed in this study, I've begun to respond with the sincere question, *"How much* prayer do you think is enough?"* I don't mean to be sarcastic or hostile. My intent is to stimulate healthy thought about prayer.

People misconstrue the practical power of prayer if they regard it as one of several *distinct* spiritual disciplines[1] to be kept in "balance." The criticism "too much prayer" implies that emphasizing this one spiritual discipline necessarily results in neglecting the others.

In actual practice, it doesn't. Those spiritual disciplines

are not really *distinct* from each other but highly *interrelated*. Concentrating on one of them enhances the others as well. Just as aerobic exercise strengthens muscles and bones, improves physical coordination, and sharpens the mind by enhancing cardiovascular health, devotion to prayer intensifies our worship, sharpens our understanding of Scripture, deepens our fellowship, and builds our faith, promoting spiritual stamina.

How Prayer Intensifies Worship

If you've been a Christian for very long, you have probably picked up the habit of meeting together with other Christians on Sunday mornings. But what would you honestly say if I asked you why you're so faithful in doing that? Remember now, I said "honestly," so don't speak too quickly. I'm sure you'd *like* to say, as would I, that you always go to church to worship the Lord. But how often are you and I genuinely motivated by that godly purpose?

Psalm 100 captures the highest motive for meeting with other Christians on Sundays:

> Shout joyfully to the LORD, all the earth.
> Serve the LORD with gladness;
> Come before Him with joyful singing.
> Know that the LORD Himself is God;
> It is He who has made us, and not we ourselves;
> We are His people and the sheep of His pasture.
> Enter His gates with thanksgiving,
> And His courts with praise.
> Give thanks to Him; bless His name.
> For the LORD is good;
> His lovingkindness is everlasting,
> And His faithfulness to all generations.

The psalmist is describing a heart bursting with worship. Is that the real reason *you* look forward to Sunday? Is it the reason *I* do?

Do we anticipate Sunday as a joyous, refreshing time to fix our attention on God and celebrate His presence among us? Or are we preoccupied with seeing our friends, taking care of church business, and wondering if this week we'll like the music or get anything out of the sermon? In these days when Christians have grown so accustomed to man-centered "worship," it behooves every one of us to consider such questions. And one of the best ways to consider them is through the practice of God-centered prayer.

When we adore God's attributes, give thanks for His goodness, describe His marvelous works, and submit ourselves to His Son, we lift our eyes from ourselves and fix them firmly on Him. When we confess sin and seek His cleansing forgiveness, we find that our Father is faithful to purify our hearts, minds, and souls so that we can worship Him in the ways He Himself has commanded. When we make our requests known to Him, we affirm our utter dependence on His mercy and grace. And when we seek His Spirit's help in digesting the preached truth of God's Word, we praise His unique work of indwelling, which seals our union with Christ.

Prayer thus intensifies every aspect of worship. Every God-centered worship service should be filled to the brim with it—as should our regular times of private worship.

The Role of Prayer in Bible Study

Have you ever wondered how Christians reading the very same Bible can come up with so many different ideas of what it says? I certainly have. Since I teach the Bible and am keenly aware of the "stricter judgment" associated with that task (James 3:1), I want to make sure that what I say about God's Word is true. Teaching Scripture is part of my high calling in Christ, and handling the truths of God accurately (2 Timothy 2:15) is one of my heart's most intense desires. If you too are a teacher, you know what I mean.

Teachers are not alone, however, in their need to understand Scripture. *Every* high calling in Christ requires walking in light. Peter emphasizes this when he exhorts every Christian to "sanctify Christ as Lord in your hearts, always being ready to make a defense to everyone who asks you to give an account for the hope that is in you" (1 Peter 3:15). A worthy walk is a walk we can defend before others. And always being ready to make a defense for our hope requires deep-seated assurance that we understand the truth of God rightly.

But where do we get that kind of assurance? Can we ever know positively that our understanding of Scripture is *entirely* correct? Because our minds have not yet been fully freed from the effects of the Fall (as they will be in heaven), I would have to say no, we cannot. But we *can* know positively whether we are seeking God's truth in a manner that glorifies Him. And if we are, He will faithfully bless our pursuits with the solid assurance we need to defend our hope from His Word.

Seeking truth in a way that glorifies God requires deep devotion to prayer.[2] After exhorting the Colossians to "let the word of Christ richly dwell within you" (3:16), and explaining what that would accomplish, Paul gives this reminder: "Devote yourselves to prayer, keeping alert in it with an attitude of thanksgiving" (4:2).

You may recall from lesson 7 that in a similar appeal to the Ephesians, he equated the work of the indwelling Spirit with the work of the Word (4:18–6:20). Paul caps that passage as well with a reference to prayer: "With all prayer and petition pray at all times in the Spirit, and with this in view, be on the alert with all perseverance and petition for all the saints" (6:18). Likewise in Romans 8, Paul directly relates the Spirit's role in our prayers (vv. 26–27) to our understanding of truth (vv. 5–8, 12–17; see also 1 Corinthians 2:6–16).

God knows we need help to comprehend the truth, and He has given us *the* perfect Teacher in His Holy Spirit. We should never open the Bible until we've sought His assistance in prayer, but we must never be fooled into thinking that one up-front prayer is enough. The assurance we need to make a ready defense of our hope grows out of study that's hemmed in on all sides by passionate prayers for enlightenment.

Our Lord's brother James underscores the vital role of prayer in our understanding of Scripture when he says, "If any of you lacks wisdom, let him ask of God, who gives to all men generously and without reproach, and it will be given to him" (1:5).

Perhaps we all should have imprinted on the fronts of our Bibles, *"Caution! Open with Prayer."* And perhaps we should imagine at the top of each page, *"Reading without prayer may be hazardous to your spiritual health."*

What Prayer Does for Fellowship

"Christian fellowship" is often thought of as small talk, red punch, and chocolate chip cookies. Although true fellowship does engage in some small talk, chokes down its fair share of red punch, and rarely refuses a good chocolate chip cookie, it calls the children of God to pursue much deeper relationships.

Biblical fellowship involves encouraging one another and stimulating each other to love and good deeds (Hebrews 10:24–25). It means being devoted to one another in brotherly love, giving preference to one another in honor (Romans 12:10), rejoicing with those who rejoice, weeping with those who weep (v. 15), refraining from playing favorites (v. 16; James 2:1), and giving sacrificially toward the genuine needs in the body (1 John 3:17–18).

True fellowship requires diligent work to preserve the unity of the Spirit in the bond of peace (Ephesians 4:3). That work includes laying aside falsehood and instead speaking the truth (v. 25); dealing with anger (v. 26); doing productive labor in order to share (v. 28); speaking words full of grace that edify others (v. 29); and remaining tenderhearted, forgiving, and kind to each other (v. 32).

Such fellowship grows as people are of the same mind, maintain the same love, and are united in spirit and intent on one purpose (Philippians 2:2). As they follow Christ's example of doing nothing from selfishness or empty conceit, they learn to place others' interests ahead of their own (vv. 3–5), and they seek to do all things without grumbling or disputing (v. 14). The growing purity of their fellowship marks them as "blameless and innocent, children of God above reproach in the midst of a crooked and perverse generation, among whom [they] appear as lights in the world" (v. 15).

These few examples present a much different definition of "Christian fellowship" than many of us are used to. But Scripture does more than simply define fellowship. It also calls us to do it. And the most difficult thing about practicing biblical fellowship is that we must work it out in our daily contacts with *people*—some of whom we don't like and would prefer to ignore. But since God won't allow us to apply Scripture selectively, we must pursue true biblical fellowship through the equipping power of prayer.

Prayerful adoration and thanksgiving remind us that God's purpose for fellowship far surpasses our personal preferences. Prayerful confession of our sins against brothers and sisters breaks down barriers between us. Prayer for the needs of other believers (with as much fervor as, if not more than, for our own) strengthens our bond of fellowship with them.

As long as we live on earth, our "people encounters" will remain imperfect and difficult. But because God's Spirit lives within us, we can strive toward God's ideal for relationships if we undergird them with prayer.

Prayer Builds Up Our Faith

Do you have a terrible time defining *faith* even though you're sure you know what it is? If so, may I suggest that you memorize Hebrews 11:1? There is no better definition of faith than the one God gives us there: "Now faith is the substance of things hoped for, the evidence of things not seen" (NKJV).

Space won't allow us to study this intriguing verse in detail or to delve into the illustrative examples of faith in the rest of Hebrews 11. But I want to note two key facts about faith: (1) It has to do with the substance (assurance grounded in reality) of our hope. (2) It involves evidence (reliable proof) of things we can't see.

God's definition of faith removes it far from the realm of irrational leaps in the dark. We may not always see where our Spirit-lit path turns, dips, or ends, but God always gives us enough light for our next step. Faith walks through this world one lighted step at a time and trusts God with the hidden turns, dips, and end.

God's definition of faith also removes it far from the realm of impractical, speculative concepts. Christian belief is based on fact. The evidence for God's intervention in history is abundant and clear, and the truth of His revelation in Scripture cannot be disproved. The faith that saves sinners is never a dreamy illusion. It is the solid foundation that supports every aspect of life.

Christian faith starts out small and grows strong with use. Each time we trust God and see Him respond in loving perfection, our faith grows more solid. Prayer is an essential part of that process. It provides us with specific occasions to watch God at work in our lives and the world. When we adore God in prayer, our understanding of Him matures, expanding our horizons beyond our short-sightedness. We further appreciate His sovereign ordaining of circumstances to fulfill His ultimate purposes. And prayerful adoration strengthens our commitment to doing His will.

Confession calls us to examine our lives for all sorts of sin. Sin interferes with our useful service to God and must be cleansed. But our self-centeredness prevents us from recognizing a lot of our sin. Asking God to help us identify and confess sin will result in a thorough housecleaning!

Supplication is a virtual arena in which God displays His glory. When we ask anything according to His will, we know He will do it (1 John 5:14–15). The resulting demonstration of power glorifies Him magnificently (John 14:13) while increasing our faith.

J. C. Ryle said that "a habit of prayer is one of the surest marks of a true Christian."[3] What we have just seen about prayer building our faith supports his assertion. Do you now see how prayer is involved in fulfilling every Christian's chief end of glorifying God and enjoying Him forever? Whenever our prayers call God into action, they give Him great glory. And watching Him work gives us great joy.

Notes:

1. A spiritual discipline could be defined as a spiritual pursuit or endeavor requiring concentration and effort, and whose consistent practice enhances our ability to glorify God and enjoy Him forever.

2. See my Light for Your Path study *Turning On the Light: Discovering the Riches of God's Word* (Phillipsburg, N.J.:

P&R Publishing, 1998), for a fuller discussion of how we should pursue truth in a manner that glorifies God.

3. J. C. Ryle, *A Call to Prayer: An Urgent Plea to Enter into the Secret Place* (Laurel, Miss: Audubon Press, n.d.), 10.

Exercises

1. Explain how the spiritual disciplines are interrelated.

2. Describe several ways that prayer intensifies worship.

3. Explain the connection between prayer and the principles contained in 2 Timothy 2:15 and 1 Peter 3:15.

4. Describe true biblical fellowship. How does prayer help foster deeper relationships among Christians?

5. Define faith. What is the relationship of "substance" and "evidence" to faith?

6. List and explain several ways prayer builds up our faith.

Application

1. *Open-Book Prayer:* This week in your prayer time, use Psalm 100, 1 Peter 3:15–16, Romans 12, and Hebrews 11 to help you better appreciate the pervasive power of prayer in your life.

2. Describe three (or more) ways this study has changed how you pray. These may come from any of the lessons. Then explain how these changes will enhance your

ability to fulfill your chief end of glorifying God and enjoying Him forever.

Digging Deeper

1. Do you believe the actual "clock hours" a person spends in prayer is a good indication of the priority he or she places on prayer? Do you believe it is a good indication of how effectively he or she prays? Explain, supporting your explanation with Scripture.

What Must I Do to Be Saved?

A strange sound drifted through the Philippian jail as midnight approached. The sound of human voices—but not the expected groans of the two men who had earlier been beaten with rods and fastened in stocks. Rather, the peaceful singing of praises to their God.

While the other prisoners quietly listened to them, the jailer dozed off, content with the bizarre calm generated by these two preachers, who, hours before, had stirred up so much commotion in the city.

Suddenly a deafening roar filled the prison as the ground began to shake violently. Sturdy doors convulsed and popped open. Chains snapped and fell at prisoners' feet. Startled into full wakefulness, the jailer stared at the wide-open doors and realized his prisoners' certain escape guaranteed his own impending death. Under Roman law, jailers paid with their lives when prisoners escaped. Resolutely, he drew his sword, thinking it better to die by his own hand than by Roman execution.

"Stop! Don't harm yourself—we are all here!" a voice boomed from the darkened inner cell. The jailer called for lights and was astonished to discover his prisoners standing quietly amid their broken chains. Trembling, he rushed in and fell at the feet of the two preachers. As soon as he was able, he led them out of the prison and asked, "Sirs, what must I do to be saved?"

— — —

In the entire history of the world, no one has ever asked a more important question. The jailer's words that night may well have been motivated by his critical physical need, but the response of Paul and Silas addressed his even more critical spiritual need: "Believe in the Lord Jesus, and you shall be saved, you and your household" (Acts 16:31).[1]

If you have never "believed in the Lord Jesus," your spiritual need, just like the jailer's, is critical. As long as your life is stained with sin, God cannot receive you into His presence. The Bible says that sin has placed a separation between you and God (Isaiah 59:2). It goes on to say that your nature has been so permeated by sin that you no longer have any desire to serve and obey God (Romans 3:10–12); therefore, you are not likely to recognize or care that a separation exists. Your situation is truly desperate because those who are separated from God will spend eternity in hell.

Since sinful hearts are unresponsive to God, the only way sinners can be saved from their desperate situation is for God to take the initiative. And this He has done! Even though all men and women deserve the punishment of hell because of their sin, God's love has prompted Him to save some who will serve Him in obedience. He did this by sending His Son, the Lord Jesus Christ, to remove the barrier of sin between God and His chosen ones (Colossians 2:13–14).

What is there about Jesus that enables Him to do this? First of all, He is God. While He was on earth, He said, "He who has seen Me has seen the Father" (John 14:9), and "I and the Father are one" (John 10:30). Because He said these things, you must conclude one of three things about His true identity: (1) He was a lunatic who believed He was God when He really wasn't; (2) He was a liar who was willing to die a hideous death for what He knew was a lie; or (3) His words are true and He is God.

Lunatics don't live the way Jesus did, and liars don't die the way He did, so if the Bible's account of Jesus' life and words is true, you can be sure He *is* God.

Since Jesus is God, He is perfectly righteous and holy. God's perfect righteousness and holiness demands that sin be punished (Ezekiel 18:4), and Jesus' perfect righteousness and holiness qualified Him to bear the punishment for the sins of those who will be saved (Romans 6:23). Jesus is the only human who never committed a sin; therefore, the punishment He bore when He died on the cross could be accepted by God as satisfaction of His justice in regard to the sins of others.

If someone you love commits a crime and is sentenced to die, you may offer to die in his place. However, if you have also committed crimes worthy of death, your death cannot satisfy the law's demands for your crimes *and* your loved one's. You can only die in his place if you are innocent of any wrongdoing.

Since Jesus lived a perfect life, God's justice could be satisfied by allowing Him to die for the sins of those who will be saved. Because God is perfectly righteous and holy, He could not act in love at the expense of justice. By sending Jesus to die, God demonstrated His love *by acting to satisfy His own justice* (Romans 3:26).

Jesus did more than die, however. He also rose from the dead. By raising Jesus from the dead, God declared that He had accepted Jesus' death in the place of those who will be saved. Because Jesus lives eternally with God, those for whom Jesus died can be assured they will also spend eternity in heaven (John 14:1–3). The separation of sin has been removed!

Ah, but the all-important question remains unanswered: What must *you do* to be saved? If God has sent His Son into the world for sinners, and Jesus Christ has died in their place, what is left for you to do? You must respond in faith to what God has done. This is what Paul meant when he told the jailer, "Believe in the Lord Jesus, and you shall be saved."

Believing in the Lord Jesus demands three responses from you: (1) an understanding of the facts regarding your hopeless sinful condition and God's action to remove the sin barrier that separates you from Him; (2) acceptance of those facts as true and applicable to you; and (3) a willingness to trust and depend upon God to save you from sin. This involves willingly placing yourself under His authority and acknowledging His sovereign right to rule over you.

But, you say, how can I do this if sin has eliminated my ability to know and appreciate God's work on my behalf? Rest assured that if you desire to have the sin barrier that separates you from God removed, He is already working to change your natural inability to respond. He is extending His gracious offer of salvation to you and will give you the faith to receive it.

If you believe God is working to call you to Himself, read the words He has written to you in the Bible (begin with the book of John in the New Testament) and pray that His Holy Spirit will help you understand what is written there. Continue to read and pray until you are ready to *repent,* that is, to turn away from sin and commit yourself to serving God.

Is there any other way you can be saved? God Himself says no, there is not. The Bible He wrote says that Jesus is the only way the sin barrier between you and God can be removed (John 14:6; Acts 4:12). He is your hope, and He is your *only* hope.

If you have questions or need any help in this matter, please write to The Evangelism Team, Providence Presbyterian Church, P. O. Box 14651, Albuquerque, NM 87191, before the day is over. God has said in His Bible that a day of judgment is coming, and after that day no one will be saved (Acts 17:30–31; 2 Thessalonians 1:7–9). The time to act is now.

Notes

1. See Acts 16:11–40 for the full biblical account of these events.

What Is the Reformed Faith?

"The Reformed faith"[1] can be defined as a theology that describes and explains the sovereign God's revelation of His actions in history to glorify Himself by redeeming selected men and women from the just consequences of their self-inflicted depravity.

It is first and foremost *theology* (the study of God), not *anthropology* (the study of humanity). Reformed thinking concentrates on developing a true knowledge of God that serves as the necessary context for all other knowledge. It affirms that the created world, including humanity itself, cannot be accurately understood apart from its relationship with the Creator.

The Reformed faith describes and explains God's revelation of Himself and His actions to humanity; it does not consist of people's attempts to define God as they wish. The Reformed faith asserts that God has revealed Himself in two distinct ways. He reveals His existence, wisdom, and power through the created universe—a process known as *natural revelation* (Romans 1:18–32); and He reveals His requirements and plans for mankind through His written Word, the Bible—a process known as *special revelation* (2 Timothy 3:16–17).

Reformed theologians uphold the Bible as the inspired, infallible, inerrant, authoritative, and fully sufficient communication of truth from God to us. When they say the Bible is "inspired," they mean that the Bible was actually written by God through the agency of human authorship in a miraculous way that preserved the thoughts of God from any taint of human sinfulness (2 Peter 1:20–21).

When they say the Bible is infallible, they mean it is *incapable* of error, and when they say it is inerrant, they mean the Bible, *in actual fact,* contains no errors. The Bible is authoritative because it comes from God whose authority over His creation is absolute (Isaiah 46:9–10). And it is completely sufficient because it contains everything necessary for us to know and live according to God's requirements (2 Peter 1:3–4).

By studying God's revelation of Himself and His work, Reformed theologians have learned two foundational truths that structure their thinking about God's relationship with human beings: God is absolutely sovereign, and people are totally depraved.[2]

Reformed thought affirms that God, by definition, is *absolutely sovereign*—that is, He controls and superintends every circumstance of life either by direct miraculous intervention or by the ordinary outworking of His providence. Reformed theologians understand that a "god" who is not sovereign cannot be God because his power would not be absolute. Since the Reformed faith accepts the Bible's teaching regarding the sovereignty of God, it denies that *anything* occurs outside of God's control.

The Reformed faith affirms the biblical teaching that Adam was created with the ability to sin and chose to do so by disobeying a clear command of God (Genesis 3:1–7). Choosing to sin changed basic human nature and left us unable not to sin—or *totally depraved*. Total depravity does not mean that all people are as bad as they possibly could be, but that every facet of their character is tainted with sin, leaving them incapable and undesirous of fellowship with

God. The Reformed faith denies that totally depraved men and women have any ability to seek after or submit to God of their own free will. Left to themselves, totally depraved men and women will remain out of fellowship with God for all eternity.

The only way for any of these men and women to have their fellowship with God restored is for God Himself to take the initiative. And the Bible declares that He has graciously chosen to do so (John 14:16). *For His own glory,* God has chosen some of those depraved men and women to live in fellowship with Him. His choice is determined by His own good pleasure and not by any virtue in the ones He has chosen. For this reason, *grace* is defined in Reformed thought as "unmerited favor."

God accomplished the salvation of His chosen ones by sending His Son, the Lord Jesus Christ, to bear God's righteous wrath against sin so that He could forgive those He had chosen. Even though Christ's work was perfect and complete, its effectiveness is limited to those who are chosen by God for salvation. Christ would not have been required to suffer any more or any less had a different number been chosen for redemption, but the benefit of His suffering is applied only to those who are called by God to believe in Him.

All of those who are thus effectually called by God will eventually believe and be saved, even though they may resist for a time (John 6:37). They cannot forfeit the salvation they have received (John 10:27–30; Romans 8:31–39).

Reformed thought affirms the clear teaching of the Bible that salvation is by faith alone through Christ alone (John 14:6; Acts 4:12; Ephesians 2:8–9), and that our good works play no part in salvation although they are generated by it (Ephesians 2:10). Salvation transforms a person's nature, giving him or her the ability and the desire to serve and obey God. The unresponsive heart of stone is changed into a sensitive heart of flesh that responds readily to God's voice (Ezekiel 36:25–27) and desires to glorify Him out of gratitude for the indescribable gift of salvation.

Reformed thought affirms that *God works in history to redeem* His chosen ones through a series of covenants. These covenants define His law, assess penalties for breaking His law, and provide for the imputation of Jesus' vicarious fulfillment of God's requirements to those God intends to redeem.[3]

The Reformed faith affirms that we were created and exist solely to glorify God, and denies that God exists to serve us. It affirms that God acts to glorify Himself by putting His attributes on display, and that His self-glorifying actions are thoroughly righteous since He is the only Being in creation worthy of glorification. It denies that God is *primarily* motivated to act by man's needs, but affirms that all of God's actions are motivated *primarily* for His own glory.

The Reformed faith emerged as a distinct belief system during the sixteenth and seventeenth centuries when men like Luther, Calvin, Zwingli, and Knox fought against the Roman Catholic Church to restore Christian doctrine to biblical truth. These men were labeled "Reformers," but they would have been better labeled "Restorers" since their goal was to correct abuses and distortions of Christianity that were rampant in the established Roman church. Reformed thinkers since their day have sought to align their understanding of God and His actions in history as closely as possible to His revealed truth.

Notes

1. This brief overview of basic Reformed beliefs is not intended to be a full explanation of or apologetic for the

Reformed faith. For a more detailed description and analysis of the Reformed faith see: R. C. Sproul, *Grace Unknown* (Grand Rapids: Baker, 1997), Loraine Boettner, *The Reformed Faith* (Phillipsburg, N.J.: Presbyterian and Reformed, 1983), *Back to Basics: Rediscovering the Richness of the Reformed Faith,* ed. David G. Hagopian (Phillipsburg, N.J.: P&R Publishing, 1996), *The Westminster Confession of Faith* (with its accompanying catechisms), or the theological writings of John Calvin, B. B. Warfield, Charles Hodge, and Louis Berkhof.

2. Both of these truths are taught throughout the pages of Scripture; however, the sovereignty of God can be seen very clearly in Isaiah 40–60 and in Job 38–42, while human depravity is described quite graphically in Romans 3:10–18.

3. An excellent discussion of these covenants is contained in chapter 5 of R. C. Sproul, *Grace Unknown.*

APPENDIX C

A Sampling of Paul's Prayers and Prayer Requests[1]

"I would to God, that whether in a short or long time, not only you, but also all who hear me this day, might become such as I am, except for these chains" (Acts 26:29).

"I thank my God through Jesus Christ for you all, because your faith is being proclaimed throughout the whole world" (Romans 1:8).

"Thanks be to God that though you were slaves of sin, you became obedient from the heart to that form of teaching to which you were committed, and having been freed from sin, you became slaves of righteousness" (Romans 6:17–18).

"Brethren, my heart's desire and my prayer to God for them [the Israelites] is for their salvation" (Romans 10:1).

"Now I urge you, brethren, by our Lord Jesus Christ and by the love of the Spirit, to strive together with me in your prayers to God for me, that I may be delivered from those who are disobedient in Judea, and that my service for Jerusalem may prove acceptable to the saints" (Romans 15:30–31).

"I thank my God always concerning you, for the grace of God which was given you in Christ Jesus, that in everything you were enriched in Him, in all speech and all knowledge, even as the testimony concerning Christ was confirmed in you, so that you are not lacking in any gift, awaiting eagerly the revelation of our Lord Jesus Christ, who shall also confirm you to the end, blameless in the day of our Lord Jesus Christ" (1 Corinthians 1:4–8).

"But thanks be to God, who always leads us in His triumph in Christ, and manifests through us the sweet aroma of the knowledge of Him in every place" (2 Corinthians 2:14).

"But thanks be to God, who puts the same earnestness on your behalf in the heart of Titus" (2 Corinthians 8:16).

"Thanks be to God for His indescribable gift!" (2 Corinthians 9:15).

"For this reason I too, having heard of the faith in the Lord Jesus which exists among you, and your love for all the saints, do not cease giving thanks for you, while making mention of you in my prayers; that the God of our Lord Jesus Christ, the Father of glory, may give to you a spirit of wisdom and of revelation in the knowledge of Him. I pray that the eyes of your heart may be enlightened, so that you may know what is the hope of His calling, what are the riches of the glory of His inheritance in the saints, and what is the surpassing greatness of His power toward us who believe" (Ephesians 1:15–19).

"For this reason, I bow my knees before the Father, from whom every family in heaven and on earth derives its name, that He would grant you, according to the riches of His glory, to be strengthened with power through His Spirit in the inner man; so that Christ may dwell in your hearts through faith; and that you, being rooted and grounded in love, may be able to comprehend with all the saints what is the breadth and length and height and depth, and to know the love of Christ which surpasses knowledge, that you may be filled up to all the fulness of God" (Ephesians 3:14–19).

"Pray on my behalf, that utterance may be given to me in the opening of my mouth, to make known with boldness the mystery of the gospel, for which I am an ambassador in chains; that in proclaiming it I may speak boldly, as I ought to speak" (Ephesians 6:19–20).

"I thank my God in all my remembrance of you, always offering prayer with joy in my every prayer for you all, in view of your participation in the gospel from the first day until now. . . . And this I pray, that your love may abound still more and more in real knowledge and all discernment, so that you may approve the things that are excellent, in order to be sincere and blameless until the day of Christ; having been filled with the fruit of righteousness which comes through Jesus Christ, to the glory and praise of God" (Philippians 1:3–5, 9–11).

"We give thanks to God, the Father of our Lord Jesus Christ, praying always for you, since we heard of your faith in Christ Jesus and the love which you have for all the saints; because of the hope laid up for you in heaven, of which you previously heard in the word of truth, the gospel, which has come to you, just as in all the world also it is constantly bearing fruit and increasing, even as it has been doing in you also since the day you heard of it and understood the grace of God in truth" (Colossians 1:3–6).

"For this reason also, since the day we heard of it, we have not ceased to pray for you and to ask that you may be filled with the knowledge of His will in all spiritual wisdom and understanding, so that you may walk in a manner worthy of the Lord, to please Him in all respects, bearing fruit in every good work and increasing in the knowledge of God; strengthened with all power, according to His glorious might, for the attaining of all steadfastness and patience; joyously giving thanks to the Father, who has qualified us to share in the inheritance of the saints in light" (Colossians 1:9–12).

"Devote yourselves to prayer, keeping alert in it with an attitude of thanksgiving; praying at the same time for us as well, that God may open up to us a door for the word, so that we may speak forth the mystery of Christ, for which I have also been imprisoned; in order that I may make it clear in the way I ought to speak" (Colossians 4:2–4).

"We give thanks to God always for all of you, making mention of you in our prayers; constantly bearing in mind your work of faith and labor of love and steadfastness of hope in our Lord Jesus Christ in the presence of our God and Father, knowing, brethren beloved by God, His choice of you" (1 Thessalonians 1:2–4).

"And for this reason we also constantly thank God that when you received from us the word of God's message, you accepted it not as the word of men, but for what it really is, the word of God, which also performs its work in you who believe" (1 Thessalonians 2:13).

"Now may our God and Father Himself and Jesus our Lord direct our way to you; and may the Lord cause you to increase and abound in love for one another, and for all men, just as we also do for you; so that He may establish your hearts unblamable in holiness before our God and Father at the coming of our Lord Jesus with all His saints" (1 Thessalonians 3:11-13).

"Now may the God of peace Himself sanctify you entirely; and may your spirit and soul and body be preserved complete, without blame at the coming of our Lord Jesus Christ. Faithful is He who calls you, and He also will bring it to pass" (1 Thessalonians 5:23-24).

"We ought always to give thanks to God for you, brethren, as is only fitting, because your faith is greatly enlarged, and the love of each one of you toward one another grows ever greater" (2 Thessalonians 1:3).

"To this end also we pray for you always that our God may count you worthy of your calling, and fulfill every desire for goodness and the work of faith with power; in order that the name of our Lord Jesus may be glorified in you, and you in Him, according to the grace of our God and the Lord Jesus Christ" (2 Thessalonians 1:11-12).

"But we should always give thanks to God for you, brethren beloved by the Lord, because God has chosen you from the beginning for salvation through sanctification by the Spirit and faith in the truth" (2 Thessalonians 2:13).

"Now may our Lord Jesus Christ Himself and God our Father, who has loved us and given us eternal comfort and good hope by grace, comfort and strengthen your hearts in every good work and word." (2 Thessalonians 2:16-17).

"Finally, brethren, pray for us that the word of the Lord may spread rapidly and be glorified, just as it did also with you;

and that we may be delivered from perverse and evil men; for not all have faith" (2 Thessalonians 3:1–2).

"Now may the Lord of peace Himself continually grant you peace in every circumstance. The Lord be with you all!" (2 Thessalonians 3:16).

"I thank Christ Jesus our Lord, who has strengthened me, because He considered me faithful, putting me into service; even though I was formerly a blasphemer and a persecutor and a violent aggressor. . . . the grace of our Lord was more than abundant . . ." (1 Timothy 1:12–14).

"I thank God, whom I serve with a clear conscience the way my forefathers did, as I constantly remember you in my prayers night and day, longing to see you, even as I recall your tears, so that I may be filled with joy" (2 Timothy 1:3–4).

"I thank my God always, making mention of you in my prayers, because I hear of your love, and of the faith which you have toward the Lord Jesus, and toward all the saints; and I pray that the fellowship of your faith may become effective through the knowledge of every good thing which is in you for Christ's sake" (Philemon 4–6).

Notes

1. I wish to acknowledge, with heaps of gratitude, Thom Notaro's labor of love in compiling this appendix and donating it to our study. Thanks, Thom!

RECOMMENDED READING

Adams, Jay E. *From Forgiven to Forgiving.* Wheaton, Ill.: Victor, 1989.

Bennett, Arthur, ed. *The Valley of Vision: A Collection of Puritan Prayers and Devotions.* Carlisle, Pa.: Banner of Truth, 1975.

Brown, Steve. *Approaching God: How to Pray.* Nashville: Moorings, 1996.

Edwards, Jonathan. *Sinners in the Hands of an Angry God.* Phillipsburg, N.J.: P&R Publishing, 1996.

Lloyd-Jones, D. Martyn. *Spiritual Depression: Its Causes and Its Cure.* Grand Rapids: Eerdmans, 1965.

MacArthur, John, Jr. *Alone with God.* Wheaton, Ill.: Victor, 1995.

―――. *The Freedom and Power of Forgiveness.* Wheaton, Ill: Crossway, 1998.

Packer, J. I. *Evangelism and the Sovereignty of God.* Downers Grove, Ill.: InterVarsity Press, 1961.

―――. *Knowing God.* Downers Grove, Ill.: InterVarsity Press, 1973.

Pink, A. W. *Gleanings from Paul: The Prayers of the Apostle.* Chicago: Moody Press, 1967.

―――. *A Guide to Fervent Prayer.* Grand Rapids: Baker, 1981.

Pipa, Joseph A. *The Root and Branch.* Philadelphia: Great Commission, 1989.

Pratt, Richard L. *Pray with Your Eyes Open.* Phillipsburg, N.J.: Presbyterian and Reformed, 1987.

Ryle, J. C. *A Call to Prayer: An Urgent Plea to Enter into the Secret Place.* Laurel, Miss.: Audubon Press, n.d.

———. *Holiness: Its Nature, Hindrances, Difficulties and Roots.* Grand Rapids: Baker, reprint 1979 (from the edition issued in 1883 by William Hunt and Company).

Sproul, R. C. *The Holiness of God.* Wheaton, Ill.: Tyndale House, 1985, 1998.

———. *The Invisible Hand: Do All Things Really Work for Good?* Dallas: Word, 1996.

Carol J. Ruvolo has been teaching the Bible since 1983 and writing books on biblical themes since 1998. A long-time resident of Albuquerque, she now speaks at women's conferences and retreats around the country.

Before the Throne of God: Focus on Prayer is the fourth in Ruvolo's Light for Your Path series, her seventh book overall. She has written more than ten volumes, including three on the Book of James.

Ruvolo earned B.S. and M.B.A. degrees from the University of New Mexico. Since 1996 she has taken graduate-level courses at Greenville Presbyterian Theological Seminary and several courses from Ligonier Ministries of Canada's School of Theology.

Though a devoted church-goer from childhood, she did not experience God's saving grace until she was an adult. Soon after her conversion she quit her job at a national defense laboratory and began devoting her time to raising her daughter and studying the Scriptures.

During the two years she participated in Bible Study Fellowship, she taught for the first time and soon realized that teaching is her spiritual gift. She says, "I have been teaching, counseling, discipling, and writing about God's revealed truth ever since."

Carol is married and has one child.